MW01170399

Make Room *for* Scripture

Make Room for Scripture

An invitation to catechists and teachers

JAMES PHILIPPS

To each and every believer,
both inside the classroom and outside of it,
who cooperates with the desire of the Spirit
to give the gifts of faith, hope, and love
to our children

TWENTY-THIRD PUBLICATIONS
A Division of Bayard
One Montauk Avenue, Suite 200
New London, CT 06320
(860) 437-3012 or (800) 321-0411
www.23rdpublications.com

Copyright ©2010 James Philipps. All rights reserved. No part of this publication may be reproduced in any manner without prior written permission of the publisher. Write to the Permissions Editor.

The Scripture passages contained herein are from the *New Revised Standard Version of the Bible*, copyright ©1989, by the Division of Christian Education of the National Council of Churches in the U.S.A. All rights reserved.

ISBN 978-1-58595-775-0
Library of Congress Catalog Card Number: 2010920813
Printed in the U.S.A.

Contents

PART VI: The Luminous Mysteries of the Rosary

Epilogue

Acknowledgments

I am grateful to Gwen Costello and Alison Berger for the opportunity to write for *Religion Teachers Journal*, for their editing skills, which always made me sound smarter and more insightful than my first drafts did, and for their continued encouragement. Thank you, Dan Connors, for the opportunity to continue my long-standing association with Bayard/Twenty-Third Publications. I am proud to be associated with a community of editors and authors who consistently produce publications that are Spirit-filled, doctrinally sound, and pastorally oriented. Blessed Pope John XXIII must be pleased.

Thanks to Dan Smart and Kerry Moriarty for all of your help in marketing my books and in responding to my questions and requests so promptly and effectively. I am grateful to all those who helped guide this book through the editing and proofreading process, in particular Michelle Gerstel.

Finally, thanks to my wife, Rosalie, for holding down the fort at home so that I could find the hours I needed to put this book together and for her ongoing encouragement. Thanks to my daughter and son for their inspiration, honest critiques of my work, and, most of all, just for being themselves. I love you all.

Introduction

Before they were recognized as the Word of God, the accounts that made their way into the Bible were preserved and passed along because they were great stories. All of the elements that make for a riveting story—heroism, villainy, the triumph of the human spirit, and, yes, even sexual escapades (see 2 Samuel 11)—are contained within the pages of the Bible. We meet a parade of saints and sinners (often the same people!) who encounter a God they only dimly understand and often misinterpret. Yet all of these stories coming together from so many different ages and cultures and representing so many different genres unite in one glorious proclamation: We are caught up within a relationship with a God who is passionately in love with each of us and who simply cannot rest easy until we extend that same passionate love to one another.

In this book, I am inviting you to look again at this most unique library of books with new eyes. Perhaps I should say with "old" eyes—the eyes of our ancestors in the faith who embraced these stories as the basis for worship and as their inspiration for living. Imagine generations of families gathered around campfires listening with rapt attention to the storytellers, or mothers gently rocking their children to sleep with reassuring tales of God's never ending love and protection. Consider the parables of Jesus as the captivating and sometimes brilliantly subversive vignettes they are intended to be. The "metanoia" they aimed to generate in the heart of the listener is often translated as "repentance" but literally means "to turn around one's mind" and see things from a whole new perspective.

In an effort to scrape away some of the layers of overly pious varnish and to invite you into a deeper connection with the stories of the Bible, the first section of this book presents brief explanations and illustrations of some basic concepts the reader needs to keep in mind so as not to miss a story's power. The next four sections are all about the stories. Contained within them you will find tales about the famous and not so famous but always extraordinary women and men of the Old and New Testament whose encounters with God leave them—and the world around them—forever changed. Next comes a collection of some of Jesus' most intriguing parables. Finally, a few stories from the Acts of the Apostles and one from the book of Revelation along with a glimpse into the mind of the greatest storyteller in Christian history: Saint Paul. It was Paul's "story" of God's love, not just for Jews but for all human beings, expressed in all its fullness in the life, death, and resurrection of Jesus Christ, that opened a small Jewish sect to the world. The book's final section is a reverent look at the scriptural basis of that storytelling tool that has caught generations of Christians in its power for at least a millennium—the rosary. In particular, the reflections focus on those "mysteries of light," which tell the story of the ministry of Jesus Christ.

Each brief reflection contains three parts: 1) a bit of Catholic Bible scholarship to help you place the story within its proper context; 2) a reflection that offers you a possible entry point into a deeper experience of the story and its transformative power; and 3) a series of questions and activities aimed at helping you to make personal connections between your life and the story and to help others do the same. While this book can be used profitably by a general Catholic audience, it is primarily for catechists and teachers. I must confess to a soft spot in my heart for those laboring in the fields of religious education, as I have been for more than twenty-five years. For these faith-filled, dedicated teachers who care deeply about children and are enthusiastic about sharing their faith but for whom time is a precious commodity, these brief reflections can provide a quick "hit" of Scripture in the classroom.

To overlook the Scriptures has the same effect as neglecting the Eucharist—one of the two legs of a healthy Catholic spiritual life is broken. Yet despite the great advances since the Second Vatican Council in making the Scriptures accessible to the faithful, many still feel a bit intimated by the words "Scripture study." Sadly, the influence of fundamentalist interpretations of the Bible is so pervasive that many Catholics are more familiar with these narrow interpretations that kill the story and turn it into a doctrinal proof text or, worse, a weapon. The best antidote to this disease is the stories themselves, which are the catalysts for communal and personal encounters between the reader and the living Word of God.

Enjoy the book. Any comments or reflections of your own you'd like to share with me would be much appreciated. I can be reached at: jimphilipps@juno.com.

PART I

Keys to Reading the Bible

The Bible was not created in a vacuum. The poems, songs, prophecies, and narratives that make up the books of the Old and New Testaments were all formed and shaped within real human communities guided by the inspiration of the Holy Spirit. These first chapters lay out essential principles for interpreting the Bible based on the teaching of the Catholic Church.

For a more in-depth development of the principles outlined in these columns, please see my book-length works: *Unlocking the Treasures of the Bible* and *Understanding the Bible* (part of the *JumpStarts for Catechists* series from Twenty-Third Publications).

1

Making the Bible
User-Friendly

What is the full name of Mrs. Noah? How many times does God create the world? How do the Hebrews celebrate their victory over the people of Jericho? The answers to these questions demonstrate why an uninformed reading of the Bible is worse than no reading at all. In this first chapter we'll begin focusing on the basic tools you need to clear away the obstacles that might prevent your students from fully experiencing the Word of God in all of its liveliness and relevance.

We never do get the name of Noah's wife, or Lot's wife for that matter. Although King David and Solomon are reputed to have had many wives, almost none of them are mentioned by name. Even when women do rate that small dignity, they generally remain in the margins of the biblical narrative. Try and find Sarah's reaction to Abraham's near sacrifice of their son Isaac, for example (Genesis 22).

Four Keys

While the second question—How many times does God create the world?—might seem like a trick, it isn't. Read Genesis 1, and you'll be taken beyond the boundaries of space and time as God goes about creating the universe according to a careful six-day plan. Human beings—both male and female—are the final masterpiece of God's labors.

Read Genesis 2 and creation begins all over again. This time, however, God makes "the man" (*Adam*, in Hebrew) first and then goes about furnishing the Garden over an indeterminate amount of time. Only then does God put the man to sleep to create the woman. Contradictions within the stories themselves and between these stories and our modern understanding of the universe abound throughout the stories of Genesis 1—11.

When the Hebrew army overruns the city of Jericho (Joshua 6), God's chosen people observe "the ban"—an order from God to kill all human beings who worship pagan gods (Leviticus 27:29). Every man, woman, child, and animal in the town is slaughtered. This famous account immortalized in the hymn "Joshua Fought the Battle of Jericho," therefore, is a story of genocide sanctioned by God. It is not the first or the last time God is portrayed this way in the Old Testament.

The good news is that these stories and many others can be read, studied, and taught in a sensible, engaging, and faith-filled way. All that is required is a thoughtful and prayerful understanding of the Bible as God's Word mediated through faithful but fractured human beings. Future chapters will present four "keys"—basic principles that are essential to a proper Catholic understanding of Scripture. In light of those principles, we'll also take a brief overview of both the Old and New Testaments.

For Thought and Discussion

1. What are some particular stories or passages in the Bible that inspire you? make you think? trouble you?

2. How comfortable are you teaching about the Bible? If you are uncomfortable, why? If you are comfortable, what is it that you find most meaningful in your teaching?

3. Do you ever read the Bible on your own? Why or why not?

4. Does the idea that every word in the Bible may not be literally true bother you? Do you see it as a challenge to your faith? If yes, why? If no, how does it help you appreciate the Bible more? (Read Raymond Brown's *101 Questions About the Bible* for a good introduction to the modern Catholic approach to Bible study.)

5. Begin the year by asking your students to share their favorite stories or characters from the Bible. Ask them what they like about the stories and ask them to explain what they think the stories mean. Look for common insights and misunderstandings that you can address in this and future lessons.

6. Read a particularly vivid story from the Bible and ask each student to draw a picture of a key scene as he or she imagines it. (Luke offers some wonderful stories to get you started—the story of the Annunciation (Lk 1:26–38) or the parable of the prodigal son (Lk 15:11–32), for example. If it's a group in which boys predominate, try the story of David and Goliath (1 Sam 17:12–50). Best to leave out verse 51!

7. Read your favorite children's book to your class. Ask your students to explain the lesson the story teaches and to comment on images or characters that they really like. Try and make some connections to specific characters, stories, and lessons in the Bible.

8. *Veggie Tales* are a series of videotapes that use humor—and vegetables!—to tell the stories of the Bible. With older children, you might have the students read the biblical story the tape is based on (e.g., "David and the Giant Pickle"/David and Goliath) and compare and contrast the two.

2

The Bible
Is a Library

Although its name belies the fact—Bible comes from the Greek *biblios* which means book—the Bible is really a library. Within the Bible's covers are works of many literary genres whose origins span thousands of years of human history. The cultures, perspectives, and writing talents of the authors who wrote them are as varied as the books themselves. While it is true that books of the Bible present the fullness of God's written revelation to the Church, this overall unity is a divine plan, not a human one.

Consider two examples, one concerning the time span and one concerning the types of books you can find in the Bible. The consensus of Catholic Bible scholars is that the last books of the New Testament were composed somewhere around the close of the first century AD. By contrast, the story of Noah's Ark has clear connections with an ancient Babylonian creation account that existed before 2000 BC!

Comparing Three Books

If you thumb through the prophets, you'll find the book of Jonah tucked neatly between the books of Obadiah and Micah. Take a closer look at the three books, however, and you'll see that the books of Obadiah and Micah consist entirely of the two men's prophetic utterances written in the form of poetry. The book of Jonah is in the form of a short story. The reason: Jonah is a fictional character, and the book of Jonah is a marvelous satire that points out the absurdity of a "God loves me more than God loves you" attitude.

The story begins with Jonah acting in a most unprophet-like manner. God calls him to deliver a message calling for the repentance of the people of Nineveh, Israel's despised enemy. In response, Jonah hops on the first boat he can find going in the opposite direction. After a dramatic series of misadventures, Jonah's a changed man and goes to Nineveh, preaching God's call for repentance. Jonah's openness to God is short-lived, however. The book closes with Jonah still struggling to accept the truth that God's love transcends human divisions.

A Change in Thinking

We need to change our way of thinking about the Bible for two reasons. As was suggested in chapter 1, the Bible contains some real inconsistencies. If the Bible is a library, then these inconsistencies are more easily explained. Putting two books next to each other on a library shelf means they share a subject in common—in the case of the biblical library that subject would be Divine Revelation—but not necessarily the same point of view.

Second, it's reasonable to assume that an author's understanding of his or her subject remains the same from the first chapter of a book to the last. A library such as the Bible, however, contains books written many centuries apart. Is it hard to believe that over thousands of years, human experience of God would change our understanding of who God is and how God works? Certainly God does not change, but human beings and our limited abilities to understand spiritual mysteries do.

For Thought and Discussion

1. On a scale of 1-10 (with 1 being the lowest and 10 the highest) rate the impact the Bible has had on influencing your image of God. What are the particular reasons for the rating that you gave? How could the Bible have greater relevance in your life?

2. In what significant ways has your image of God changed over the years? What major questions about God are you struggling with at this time?

3

Inspiration
Is Not Dictation

God is the author of the Bible. This does not mean that God wrote the Bible, however. When we say that the Bible is inspired by God, we do not mean that the Holy Spirit was a boss dictating to a group of stenographers. If this were the case, any attempts to interpret the words of the Bible—even to translate the books of the Bible from their original languages—would be foolish. The mark of a good stenographer is his or her ability to get the boss's words exactly right.

The Church defines biblical inspiration this way: "To compose the sacred books (of the Bible), God chose certain men who, all the while he employed them in this task, made full use of their powers and faculties so that, though he acted in them and by them, it was as true authors that they consigned to writing whatever he wanted written, and no more" (*Dei Verbum*, sect. 11). To say that the writers of the books of the Bible were "true authors" is to say that the books of our biblical library reflect the distinct abilities of their human authors—as well as their limitations.

How, then, can we be sure that these fallible human authors faithfully communicated to us "that truth which God, for the sake of our salvation, wished to see confided to the sacred Scriptures" (*Dei Verbum*, sect. 11)? Closely related to the Catholic understanding of biblical inspiration is our belief in biblical inerrancy: The Holy Spirit guarantees that the Bible can never be in error when it presents religious truth. The biblical authors' perspectives on the nature of the world and human society may or may not stand up to a modern critical examination. The truth about God and God's relationship to us, however, is timeless and unchanging.

A Proper Understanding of Inspiration

Consider once again that first Creation story in Genesis 1. If we look at the myth through the lens of our modern scientific understanding of the natural world we run into a number of factual errors in the story. It took billions of years for complex life to evolve on our planet, not six days. Certainly the creation of woman from man in the second creation story (Genesis 2) violates all known laws of biology.

And yet the profound religious truths of the story remain firm. Creation was not an accident, but a carefully planned process totally under the initiative of God. The revelation that the meaning and purpose of our lives is grounded in the creative and unconditional love of God remains as true today as it was thousands of years ago when the Creation stories first took their shape.

A proper understanding of inspiration allows us the freedom to become the guides into the Scriptures that our students desperately need. We can confidently use modern analogies and ways of thinking to help our youngsters grasp the profound spiritual insights the stories of the Bible contain. In Scripture study, as in all things, we are called to be active partners with the Holy Spirit in the search for truth and meaning and not merely to be passive and unimaginative servants.

For Thought and Discussion

1. Spend some time looking at the unique approaches to the story of Jesus' birth found in the gospels of Matthew and Luke (Luke 1—2; Matthew 1—2). Have the students draw or describe the different descriptions of the events.

2. Ask your class to come up with as many uses of the word "inspiration" as possible. (Example: "That quarterback played like he was inspired today.") How do these definitions compare to and contrast with the Church's definition of biblical inspiration?

3. Read the story of Noah's Ark (Genesis 6—9) or the Tower of Babel (Genesis 11). Ask your students to point out the details that seem fanciful. What truth about faith can we take from the struggles of Noah and his family? (Let your students design their own arks or towers with building blocks.)

4. How have you experienced the partnership with the Holy Spirit in your life? What events and memories demonstrate the hand of God at work in your life?

5. What are the stories in the Bible that you wonder about the most? Can you find a meaningful lesson or insight for your own life in the story? Which facts in the story led you to this deeper insight?

4

Read Contextually

The other day my daughter asked me if I could go into the backyard and find her blue pony. If she hadn't mentioned that she needed it for her hair, I might have been out there a long time looking for a toy horse rather than the "scrunchie" she uses to make a pony-tail. Each of us makes adjustments in our interpretation of another person's words based on context clues all of the time. We would become confused if we didn't, because most messages we send and receive are conveyed at least as much by non-verbal communication as they are by words.

People often think that the Bible is exempt from the need to read things in context. They assume that if the reader doesn't interpret the words of Scripture in the most literal way possible, then he or she will distort their meaning. If we need to rely on contextual clues to understand the meaning of our own lives, however, then why wouldn't we need to do so when we're trying to make sense of books created by communities separated from us by vast amounts of time and significantly different views of the world?

The Sermon on the Mount (Matthew 5—7) is the most eloquent and comprehensive expression of Christian moral teaching in the gospels. In chapter 5, the following two statements are attributed to Jesus:

> "If your right eye causes you to sin, tear it out and throw it away. It is better for you to lose one of your members than to have your whole body thrown into Gehenna." (v. 29)

> "You have heard that it was said, 'You shall love your neighbor and hate your enemy.' But I say to you, love your enemies, and pray for those who persecute you." (v. 43–44)

Literal or Exaggerated?

How should these statements be understood? Are we to take both of them literally and preach bodily mutilation? Or can we consider them both to be figures of speech and thus water down that ridiculously difficult command about loving enemies so that it means, "Try and be nice to everyone"? What context clues can help us here?

Prophets of the Old Testament made great use of hyperbole—a figure of speech that uses exaggeration to capture the listener's attention. So when Jesus, the ultimate prophet, speaks of gouging out eyes and cutting off hands, he's trying to help his listeners appreciate just how essential it is to place God first.

Jesus' life, and especially his death, present us with a clear witness to how literally he wishes us to take the second statement, however. Even as Jesus is dying with his tormentors standing around and mocking him, Jesus prays, "Father, forgive them, they know not what they do" (Luke 23:34). Simply being nice just isn't going to cut it.

Understanding the basic context clues you need to make your way through most Bible stories does not require an advanced degree in Scripture studies. All you need is an openness to the Word of

God and a good modern translation of the Bible with commentary. You will soon see the fruits of your labors as your students learn to see the Bible not as a faded, two-dimensional picture of God but as a three-dimensional portal through which they can meet the living God who has loved them into life.

For Thought and Discussion

1. Help students get a sense of the context in which the stories in the Bible were written by devoting a class or two each year to "biblical times" days. Some sample themes: foods that Jesus and his family and friends ate; how people made a living in 30 AD; ancient Jewish celebrations, such as weddings and banquets. These theme days could include costumes, art work, "show and tell" items, sample foods, music, and perhaps skits.

2. Use examples of taking things out of context (e.g., when we overhear only part of a conversation, or when a news article quotes only part of what a person says).

3. Give yourself a present and buy a copy of the *Catholic Youth Bible* (*New American Bible* version from St. Mary's Press). Pick a Bible story you are familiar with and write down as much as you can remember about the story from memory. Also write down the meaning of the story as you have always understood it and any questions you may have about the story's details.

    Now read the story and any background notes available in the *Catholic Youth Bible*. What new information did you learn? Did you find the answers to any of your questions? How has this contextual information affected your understanding of the religious truth within this story?

5

Oral Tradition

"Oral tradition" is the passing on of stories from one generation to the next by word of mouth. It is important to understand how this process works because the Bible texts we read are often the end products of centuries of oral transmission. Some of the oldest portions of the Bible—the story of the Garden of Eden, for example—have roots that go back at least as far as the third millennium BC. The written version of the Hebrew Scriptures that formed the basis for the Catholic Old Testament was not composed until thousands of years later—just several hundred years before the birth of Jesus. Even the gospels are removed from the life and times of Jesus himself by two or three generations.

Oral tradition is extremely good at boiling a story down to its essential truth. Intended both to entertain and instruct, stories in oral tradition exaggerate heroic deeds and punch up the drama of a story. Most likely more than one version of a particular tale is in circulation at the same time during the period of oral transmission. Finally, oral tradition tends to make great use of songs and poems that are easy to remember but tend to lack specific details of historical events.

The Exodus Drama

Anyone who has seen *The Ten Commandments* or *The Prince of Egypt* knows the dramatic power of Exodus 14—15. Moses leads a band of Hebrew slaves away from the Egyptian chariots with the waters of the Red Sea parted by God "like a wall to their right and to their left." Closer inspection of this story reveals the effects of oral tradition as we read about an Egyptian army that seems to be in retreat and in full charge at the same time (14:25–27).

And, although chapter 15 follows chapter 14 in the narrative, the consensus of Catholic Bible scholars is that the poem in chapter 15 is older and much more directly connected to the oral transmission phase of the story. Also note that any attempts to pinpoint the location of these events will prove futile—the phrase translated as Red Sea (literally, "sea of reeds") may not be referring to that massive body of water at all.

The relationship between the oral versions of a story in the Bible and the written version is similar to the relationship between a photograph of a person and the person herself or himself. A good photograph captures something of the individual's true character, but not everything. The stories of the Bible are particular insights into a much more complex experience of God. This realization can encourage us as catechists to push our creativity and our children's creativity to the max in making meaningful connections between the stories that nourish our faith and our lives today.

For Thought and Discussion

1. What are the stories preserved and passed along by oral tradition among your friends and family? Why are they so memorable? What important truths do they convey? What purpose do they serve in helping you understand yourself?

2. Read the account of Exodus 14—15 as a prayerful reflection. How has God dramatically intervened in your life? In what ways are you like the Hebrew slaves, yearning to be free? Where are you being challenged to have faith?

3. A tried and true method of helping youngsters get a sense of oral tradition is by playing the "Telephone Game." The simplest method is to whisper a phrase to one youngster, instructing him or her to whisper the phrase to the next child. This process continues until the last child in the row or around the table repeats the phrase out loud.

    An alternative version is to get several volunteers to play the game in front of the class. Select one youngster to begin, then send the others out of the room. Tell a story to the first child so that the entire class can hear it. Then call in one youngster from the hallway. Each of the volunteers must tell the story out loud to the next one as he or she remembers it. The last volunteer tells the story to the whole class.

    Using either method, ask the members of the class to point out specific changes that occurred between the initial story or phrase and the final version. Help youngsters focus on examples of how oral tradition eliminates or changes irrelevant details, communicates dramatic ones, and simplifies the basic message of the story.

6

Unlocking the
Old Testament

Hanging on the wall in my daughter's bedroom is a beautiful color print of one of the best known and loved stories in the book of Genesis. It depicts a boat framed by a rainbow and filled with adorable animals. A close inspection of the actual text of the story of Noah's Ark, however, may prompt such questions as these from your youngsters:

Why would a merciful and loving God ever destroy the world?

What does the story mean when it says that God opened the windows (or floodgates) of the heavens?

How many pairs of animals were actually on this boat, anyway? (Contrast verses 2–3 and 8–9 of Genesis 7.) Could any boat really be that big?

Our four keys can give us some help in dealing with these and other questions.

Key #1: The Bible Is a Library

The story of Noah's Ark in Genesis 6—9 is a good example of a myth—an imaginative story that communicates a profound truth. A myth is not based on any historical facts. It is an attempt by a particular culture to express in words its deepest experiences of God, the created world, and the human condition. God's destruction of the world by flood and the image of a humongous boat are the imaginative details. The persistent, stubborn, and ongoing concern for the human race exhibited by God in the story is the profound truth.

Key #2: Reading in Context

When we read this story in the context of an ancient Hebrew understanding of the universe, it makes perfect sense why God would start the flood by opening some kind of doorways in the sky. These ancient people believed that the chaos that existed before God created the universe was waterlogged. (Read the first few verses of Genesis 1.) One of the first things God did, therefore, was to separate "the waters above" from "the waters below" and to place the earth in this warm and dry pocket. The chaotic watery mess lay just outside the boundaries of the created universe, however, just waiting for the chance to wreak havoc.

Key #3: Inspiration

Did the writers of these early stories of Genesis truly believe in the understanding of the physical universe that they described? Quite possibly. Remember that Inspiration is a divine-human partnership. Our belief in the Bible's inerrancy assures us that the religious truth contained within the stories of the Bible is always what God wishes to communicate to us, no matter what the limitations of the human author may have been.

Key #4: Oral Tradition

The discrepancy over how many pairs of animals went into the ark is a good example of oral tradition at work. The first instruction about "clean" animals and "unclean" animals emphasizes the importance of ancient Hebrew religious ritual. (The terms "clean" and "unclean" concern an animal's value or lack of value as a ritual sacrifice to God.) The second and more well-known instruction, where Noah brings in one pair of every kind of animal, was contained in another version of the story that could have existed alongside or even developed before the first example.

All of the particular background details mentioned above can be found in any good modern translation of the Bible. So pick your favorite story and in the spirit of prayerful discernment, dive into the Bible. The water (pun intended) really is fine.

For Thought and Discussion

1. How has your "worldview" changed in significant ways over the course of your life? Consider your views on: God, happiness, success, love, teaching, yourself. What are some of the quantum leaps you've made? Where might you be trapped by some false conclusions you have drawn?

2. A good Easter reflection: As a result of your work with the four keys, are there any concepts concerning the Bible you have put to rest? What new ideas or insights have arisen in your mind to take their place?

3. Spend a class helping your youngsters familiarize themselves with the background resources contained within their Bibles. Depending on the translations you have available, these resources might include: background articles, footnotes, cross-references, maps, glossaries, indexes, and bibliographies.

4. Younger children can make posters illustrating the four keys in whatever imaginative ways you and your group can come up with. (You could start by giving groups of students pieces of poster board containing large key chains.)

7

Unlocking the
New Testament

According to the account found in the Acts of the Apostles, the followers of Jesus gathered together in Jerusalem have an overwhelming experience of God on that first Christian Pentecost. "And suddenly from heaven there came a sound like the rush of a violent wind....All of them were filled with the Holy Spirit" (Acts 2:1–4). The disciples immediately begin to proclaim the gospel to the crowds gathered in Jerusalem. (Pentecost originated as a Jewish feast day.) What most amazes the listeners who come from every corner of the Eastern Roman Empire is that even though they speak different languages, every member of the crowd can understand what the disciples are saying without translation (Acts 2:5–12).

Using the Four Keys

Using the four keys, what insights can we gain into this depiction of the day sometimes called the "birthday of the Church"? The first few verses of Luke's gospel and of Acts gives us an important context clue. Both works were written by the same author. (See Luke 1:1–4; Acts 1:1–5.) Taken together, Luke and Acts tell on a grand scale the story of the end of the age of prophecy, the arrival of the Messiah in the person of Jesus of Nazareth, the establishment of the Kingdom of God through Jesus' death and resurrection, and the inevitable spreading of the good news throughout the known world. Located right in the middle of this story, the Pentecost event, along with the resurrection and ascension, becomes an axis upon which the whole direction of human history turns.

Keeping in mind that the Bible is a library of books can help point us to another significant connection the author of Acts is making to an earlier book in the collection. The Pentecost account of people of many different languages coming together under the influence of God sounds very much like the story of the Tower of Babel in Genesis 3. This time, however, the plot is reversed.

In that story, one that clearly shows oral tradition at work in the exaggerated height of the tower (which reaches into the heavens) and in the image of all of the people of the world involved in the same construction project, God scrambles the languages of the builders in order to stop them from completing their foolhardy enterprise. Using the metaphor of language as a symbol for unity and disunity, the author of Acts shows God through the Pentecost event bringing human beings together once again. This time, however, they will be united in a much more magnificent construction project—the building of the Kingdom of God.

Our belief in the inspired nature of the Pentecost story assures us that the religious truth behind this spectacular intervention by the Holy Spirit holds true, whether or not the specific details of this account or of the Tower of Babel story are historical truths. Whether the disciples who gathered together on that first Christian

Pentecost left their encounter with the Spirit literally windblown and slightly singed by fire or not, the fundamental change that had taken place in the depths of their souls certainly had the power of a hurricane and a firestorm combined. As a result of their preaching and living out of the Christian life, the world would never be the same either.

For Thought and Discussion

1. As you look back over the school year, what are your "Pentecost" moments? (Those moments when you really experienced the presence of God in your teaching and in your interaction with your students.) How have these moments changed you? What are you most thankful for this year?

2. How have these chapters and your subsequent reflections aided you in your relationship and familiarity with the Bible? In what specific ways?

3. Older students can do some research on the original meaning of Pentecost, one of three principal Jewish feasts of Jesus' time along with Passover and the feast of Booths. Perhaps groups of students could report on the meaning of each feast.

4. Brainstorm about other images besides wind and fire that might be effective at communicating the power and gifts of the Holy Spirit.

5. Update the Pentecost story—the disciples of Jesus speak at the United Nations. Who would be in the audience? What would the disciples' message be for our modern times? How do your students imagine the arrival of the Holy Spirit?

PART II

Heroes and "Sheroes"
OF THE OLD TESTAMENT

As it is in life, so it is in the Bible. It is through the people we meet and with whom we form relationships that we come to know God's love and, ultimately, come to know ourselves. Every so often each one of us is blessed to meet someone who has attained such holiness in his or her own life that our respective capacities to receive God's grace and to comprehend the movement of the Holy Spirit is greatly expanded. These chapters focus on seven such holy people who, each in his or her unique way, have become major threads in the tapestry of Covenant in the Hebrew Scriptures.

Concluding this series of reflections is a chapter focusing on what is perhaps the greatest sister-and-brother act in history—Miriam and Moses.

8

Rebekah:
Making a Leap of Faith

Being a catechist means building up the Kingdom of God in a direct and profound way. We provide guidance and support as we lead children, with the help of God, to ever-deeper levels of understanding of the gospel message and into the conversion experience this understanding triggers. As we grapple with ever-limited resources and the ups and downs of human nature, however, we can sometimes lose touch with the tremendous act of empowerment we are engaged in for the sake of the Church.

These men and women we're going to look at in this section each faced tremendous limitations imposed on them by their life situations. They not only transcended these boundaries but by the grace of God actually transformed their limitations into the source of their strength. Consider, for example, Rebekah, wife of Isaac.

Rebekah's Story
Rebekah is the mother of twin boys, Esau and Jacob, and she is the wife of Isaac, the son of Abraham. Generally speaking, the

thoughts and actions of the wives of the Patriarchs are given little consideration in Genesis. In Genesis 27, however, Rebekah is the central character. Although this story is often referred to as Jacob's deception, it is Rebekah who masterminds the plot.

As the story opens, Isaac is on his deathbed, preparing to give Jacob's twin brother, Esau, the blessing that will signal the transfer of Isaac's wealth and power to his oldest son. Rebekah summons Jacob, the younger twin, and explains to him how, by impersonating his brother, he can take advantage of Isaac's failing eyesight and receive the blessing himself. Jacob fears punishment if his father discovers the ruse, and he only agrees to carry it out when his mother promises to take full responsibility before God (v. 13). When the plan works, Rebekah then has to engineer her younger son's escape to avoid his brother's wrath.

So where's the heroism here? The legends of the earliest ancestors of the Hebrew people reflect the limitations of an ancient patriarchal society where social and legal custom ensured that women remained marginalized and hidden away from the public realm. Generally speaking, this society viewed women as a unique class of property belonging to men. (Look at the traditional rendering of the ninth and tenth commandments to see a reflection of this.)

Upon the death of a patriarch, all wealth passed into the hands of the eldest son or closest surviving male relative. This was done to keep the family lands intact from one generation to the next. In the story of Jacob's deception, therefore, Rebekah is about to be trapped in a situation where her future wellbeing and financial security will be in the hands of Esau, whose only qualifications for taking on that role is the chance occurrence of having been born several minutes before Jacob.

The Best Choice

But the situation is much more serious even than this. Every story in the Hebrew Bible (Old Testament) is a thread of a tapestry that, taken as a whole, reveals the richness and diversity of the covenant relationship between God and God's people. In all of the narratives that make up the second part of the book of Genesis, the male head of the family is the particular contact point between God and the rest of the chosen people. Rebekah has discerned that it is Jacob, not Esau, whom God has selected, and she uses any and all means available to see that God's will is carried out.

Take some time to read the story yourself. The intricacies of the plot, especially the sometimes comic details of the plan that has Jacob impersonating Esau, and the terrific irony between what appears to be happening (Isaac's in charge) versus what is really going on (Rebekah's running the show) serve to make the narrative one of the most memorable in Genesis.

But how does Rebekah know that Jacob is the right choice? That's a question whose answer remains a mystery. There are glimpses of Jacob's cleverness (see Genesis 25:27–34, for example), but as Jacob flees the Promised Land after deceiving his brother and his father we see few indications of the strength and courage he will demonstrate when he returns many years later. In her decision to help Jacob, Rebekah has made a definitive leap of faith. In the midst of her seeming powerlessness, struggling against the ingrained social customs and attitudes of her times, Rebekah finds a way to be God's instrument in advancing the covenant relationship.

So if sometime during the course of this school year you find yourself absolutely stymied by a student you can't figure out, or tempted to write off a child who just doesn't seem interested or wonder if it's worth the time and effort and prayer that you expend in order to help the children in your class become more aware of the presence of Jesus in their lives, think about Rebekah's story. When we take that decisive step to unite our limited power with the unlimited power of God, miracles happen. The seeds we plant will bear great fruit as the next generation of Rebekahs and Jacobs take their rightful place among the people of the covenant fulfilled by the death and resurrection of Jesus.

For Thought and Discussion

1. Have you ever had a "Jacob" in your religion class (a child in whom you saw potential, but whom others had written off)? How did you feel when you first met this child? At the end of the year? Did you pick up any clues that you can use in identifying future Jacobs?

2. Have you ever found yourself in Rebekah's position, seemingly blocked from doing the work you felt called to do by a difficult classroom situation, overly rigid policy, or too limited resources? Does the way in which Rebekah worked out her vocation give you any insights into your own? Is there anything that you will do differently after reflecting on Rebekah's story? Why or why not?

3. What is the "leap of faith" God is calling you to make in your work as a catechist this year? Is there anything holding you back? Who are the people who encourage and inspire you?

4. What are your hopes and expectations for this new school year? Greatest fears? In what ways can you use the creativity and determination God has blessed you with to work toward your vision?

9

Deborah:
A Real Mover and Shaker

All Saints day is the feast in the Church calendar when we celebrate the witness of those holy women and men whose lives of service and intimacy with God inspire us and serve as models of genuine Christian living. The value of such modeling is that it provides us with a tangible sign of how much good can be accomplished, even in the face of daunting adversity, when we place our complete trust in God.

The story of Deborah's leadership recounted in the book of Judges is a particularly good example of a woman whose unquestioning fidelity to God enables her to transcend the limitations of her times and social station.

Deborah is introduced in chapter four of the book of Judges as a prophet and a judge. During the time in which she lived, the Israelites had begun the settlement of the promised land but were not yet a nation. The loose confederation of the twelve tribes meant that they remained autonomous from one another except in times of crisis.

During those times, the tribes relied on a charismatic figure known as a judge to act as a mediator between the people and God and to lead them into combat against any one of a number of enemies. The book of Judges is a collection of sagas about select judges and their exploits during the approximately 200-year period from the exodus to the formation of the kingdom of Israel.

The Only Female Judge

While the backgrounds of each of the judges featured in this book are quite varied, Deborah is the only woman who is described in this role. Women were generally not allowed to be involved in the public forum in a patriarchal society such as ancient Israel. The very fact that Deborah is acknowledged as a spiritual and temporal leader is a testimony to her extraordinary abilities.

We begin to gain an insight into these abilities in the first part of chapter four. The story tells us that a king of the Canaanites, the original occupants of the promised land, has conquered the tribes of Israel and placed the promised land under his domain (Judges 4:1–3). Deborah summons her general, Barak, and instructs him to engage Sisera, the commander of the enemy forces, in battle. The army of Israel seems overmatched by the 900 chariots available to Sisera, but Deborah exhorts Barak to have faith in the Lord's promise of victory.

He doesn't. "I will go if you go with me," Barak says, "but if you don't go with me, I won't go either" (v. 8). Deborah agrees to accompany him but tells him that as a result of his lack of faith "the Lord will hand Sisera over to a woman" (v. 9). This brief dialogue is significant for a couple of reasons. Barak's lack of faith is clearly chastised in Deborah's reply. This patriarchal society having to rely on a woman's help for victory in a battle would be a profound humiliation. But the account also speaks volumes about the confidence and faith that Barak and, presumably, all of the people, place in Deborah's leadership and holiness.

A Victory for Israel

Deborah gives the battle cry to Barak, and all goes as predicted. The Lord gives the Hebrew army the victory but Sisera escapes. The last part of the story (v. 17–24) shows Deborah's prophecy of the death of Sisera at the hand of a woman fulfilled in a most unexpected way. Exhausted after the day's rout, Sisera takes refuge in the tent of Jael, the wife of a local potentate whom he views as an ally. While he's sleeping, Jael drives a tent peg through his skull. The magnitude of this victory for Israel is clearly seen in the song of celebration in chapter 5, a poetic remembrance of the battle and of Deborah's leadership that pre-dates the prose account found in chapter four.

And then the prophet and judge named Deborah disappears from history. We don't know how she came to public notice. (Perhaps her husband, mentioned by name in Judges 4:4, was a prominent figure?) What happens to her after the events described is also a mystery. We do know that her absolute faith in God, which inspired and gave strength to her people in a time of grave crisis, moved the unnamed poet of Judges 5 to refer to her as "a mother for Israel" (v. 7).

The sureness of Deborah's conviction in the face of an overwhelmingly superior enemy is contrasted with the wavering conviction of the celebrated general Barak. This contrast has the power to move us to reflect on the meaning of genuine strength and on the ability of God to transform the landscape in ways unimaginable to us.

Catechetical Battles

Our "battles" as catechists are not waged against opposing armies. The forces we must combat on behalf of our students are no less overwhelming, however. In explicit and implicit ways, our students are assaulted with messages that present various forms of manipulation as models of genuine relationship, that suggest we live in an amoral universe where "moral" choices are simply those that are expedient, and that considers the idea of a personal God who cares for every individual the height of absurdity. Such dehumanizing messages and images affect our young people with all the force of the 900 iron chariots of the Canaanites. In the face of this onslaught, the calm and steady faithfulness of Deborah can inspire us to encourage one another and to just as steadily go about the business of chasing away these shadows from our students' minds by shining the light of the gospel message.

For Thought and Discussion

1. What are some of the "chariots" that are besieging those you teach? What circumstances, messages, or pressures are the greatest obstacles they face in becoming the people they want to be?

2. When faced with adversity in your ministry, either within the classroom or outside of it, do you tend to react more like Barak: looking only at your own power and feeling overmatched. Or, do you react like Deborah: with a serenity that comes from knowing God is working through you?

3. Recall a time when you responded to a stressful situation in your ministry by consciously opening yourself more to God. What was the result? What factors in the situation helped you to be more prayerful?

4. With your class, or colleagues, or by yourself, write an ending to the saga of Deborah. What happened to her after the events recounted in Judges? Invite those you teach to share their insights about this. What might they say to Deborah in a letter?

10

Elijah:
God's Quiet Voice

Christmas is too commercial! Its noise, its frantic activity, its incessant sales pitches drown out the joyous announcement of our Savior's birth. However, we can take heart from the books of the Bible where, each time the aimless noise and confusion of the world threatens to overwhelm God's people, in the end it's only the presence of God that endures. The prophet Elijah, who struggled with the external limitations of his own time, can be a powerful model for us.

Brief But Powerful Stories

The Bible stories connected with the prophet Elijah are brief but powerful. Elijah brings back to life the dead son of a widow (1 Kings 17:17–24), as Jesus would later raise the dead son of the widow of Nain. And just as Jesus of Nazareth leaves the world in a unique way, so Elijah is last seen walking with his apprentice, Elisha, when "...a flaming chariot and flaming horses came between them, and Elijah went up to heaven in a whirlwind" (2 Kings 2:11).

Just how important this prophet was in the collective memory of the people of Israel is obvious in the story of Jesus' Transfiguration in the gospels. In this account of selected apostles gaining a glimpse into the divine nature of Jesus, the transfigured Jesus is seen talking with Moses and Elijah (Mark 9:2–8).

It's only natural, therefore, that Elijah be featured in a story that contains all the elements of a legend: heroic courage, the clear triumph of good over evil, and personal touches designed to make the hero endearing as well as admirable. In the story as recounted in 1 Kings 18, Elijah, a prophet in Israel about eight centuries before the birth of Jesus, finds himself in quite a jam. Led by the example of their pagan queen, Jezebel, the people of Israel have turned in large numbers to the worship of pagan deities.

A Jolt from the Sky

Elijah is outnumbered, but he nevertheless challenges the false prophets to a showdown. Both Elijah and the false prophets build altars for sacrifice at the top of Mt. Carmel and call on their respective deities to send down fire that will consume the offering. (The practice of burning partial or entire animal carcasses—called holocausts—was a common part of many ancient religious rituals.)

Confident that Yahweh will deliver the day, Elijah allows the false prophets to call on their god first, and when their frenetic actions prove fruitless, he chimes in with mock encouragement: "Call louder...Perhaps he is asleep and must be awakened" (1 Kings 18:27). When Yahweh then responds with a jolt of fire from the sky in response to Elijah's prayer, the crowd is astounded and convinced that "The Lord is God; the Lord alone is God" (1 Kings 18:39)!

(This, by the way, is the kind of experience in my work as a catechist that I fantasize about... My unswerving faith in God rewarded in spectacular fashion as my students immediately accept the truth of what I am teaching and, by the way, realize what a magnificent teacher I happen to be!)

A Powerful Story

The next story in the Elijah cycle is one of the most powerful of all the stories centering around this prophet. When word gets back to the palace about what Elijah has done, Queen Jezebel vows to have Elijah's head. He makes a run for it into the wilderness.

After walking forty days (a symbolic number in the Bible, indicating a time of preparation or testing), he find himself at the foot of Mt. Sinai. This is the mountain on which Moses received the Ten Commandments. Clearly Elijah is ready for a special encounter with God, and he gets one.

As he stands on top of Mt. Sinai he experiences, in rapid succession, hurricane-level winds, an earthquake, and a fire—all elemental symbols of nature that in many ancient belief systems were assumed to be the ways the gods made their presence known. But God is not contained in these forces. Elijah's faith that God is present wins out over his exhaustion, hunger, and despondency, impelling him to hold out just a little longer until he finally hears the soft whisper of a voice, God's voice (1 Kings 19).

On the surface, the two stories centering on Elijah's encounters with God couldn't seem more contradictory. The first is public, in which Elijah's faith in God is rewarded in direct and spectacular fashion. The second is private, and challenges many of the ideas human beings carry around with them—then and now—about the way God is supposed to act.

And yet in both stories it is the faith of that single, power-less figure that makes God's presence known inside of time and space. Perhaps the stories about Elijah can remind us to listen ever closer to the many ways in which the still, small voice of God makes itself known to us amid all of the noise and confusion of daily life.

For Thought and Discussion

1. What are some of the surprising ways you have encountered God's presence? In particular, who are the people who have helped you encounter God in unexpected ways?

2. Think about the moments in your life when you have felt most powerful and most powerless. Which of those moments have helped to deepen and enrich your spiritual life? Why?

3. What are the particular "false gods" that you need to help your students fight against? How can you help them?

11

Jeremiah:
Taking Risks for God

"You duped me, O Lord, and I let myself be duped!" If you find your enthusiasm for teaching competing at times with feelings similar to this lament of the prophet Jeremiah (Jeremiah 20:7), don't feel too bad. We invest so much of ourselves in our ministry with our students. There will be times when exhaustion or frustration get the better of us. We can take much comfort and inspiration from the words of Jeremiah, whose ministry to the people of Judah took him from the heights of hope to the depths of despair.

The books of the Hebrew Bible (Old Testament) clearly show that the life of a prophet is a difficult one. The prophet is required to speak out on behalf of God, sometimes proclaiming a message of hope and sometimes pointing out Israel's collective failings in living out the covenant. God's messengers risk public humiliation and physical harm because their proclamations challenge popular perceptions of reality.

The Historical Setting

By the time Jeremiah comes on the scene in the late seventh century BC, the northern kingdom of the Hebrew people is long gone, obliterated from history by the mighty Assyrian army. The Southern kingdom in which Jeremiah lives (Judah) is a generation away from its own defeat at the hands of the Babylonian army from the east, an event that will begin the Exile in 587 BC Jeremiah lives to see the destruction of Jerusalem and the forced exodus of thousands of Jews into the far reaches of the Babylonian Empire.

Jeremiah began his career as a prophet sometime after 629 BC, during the reform movement within Judaism inaugurated by King Josiah. The call of the young Jeremiah is described in beautiful poetry that conveys the intimacy the prophet experienced in his relationship with God: "Before I formed you in the womb I knew you, before You were born I dedicated you...I am with you to deliver you, says the LORD" (Jeremiah 1:5, 8). The prophet begins to preach not only through words but through symbolic prophecy. This kind of prophecy involves dramatic gestures such as smashing a clay flask on the ground (to demonstrate the fate of the nation at the hands of invaders if Josiah's reforms are not carried out).

The reforms come to a grinding halt in 609 BC when Josiah is killed in battle. Probably as a result of losing his royal patron, things get ugly for Jeremiah fast. His lament to God, found in its entirety in Jeremiah 20:7–18, is placed immediately after the account of the prophet's scourging (beating) and public humiliation at the hands of the high priest in Jerusalem. But Jeremiah continues to prophesy because he must: "I say to myself, I will not mention him, I will speak God's name no more. But then it becomes like fire burning in my heart,...I cannot endure it" (Jeremiah 20:9).

Passionately in Love

Jeremiah is passionately in love with God and with God's people. In the Hebrew understanding of God, the role of the prophet was essential. Only through listening to the words of the prophet could people come to understand what faithful living according to the demands of the covenant really meant. For Jeremiah to have abandoned his role as prophet would have meant turning his back on the loving relationship that had given his nation life. So even in the midst of turmoil and suffering, the prophet continues to proclaim.

A New Covenant

"The days are coming, says the Lord, when I will make a new covenant with the house of Israel and the house of Judah...I will place my law within them, and write it upon their hearts. I will be their God, and they shall be my people" (Jeremiah 31:31, 33). In his annunciation of the "new covenant," Jeremiah hints at the divine-human intimacy that the life, death, and resurrection of Jesus will make possible.

The courage, intelligence, and vitality that marked the character of the prophet Jeremiah are unmistakable to anyone reading the Bible book that bears his name. But what ultimately enables him to see what is happening to his nation and to confront it is his passionate love. It impels him to take risks and keep going, when to do so seems the height of absurdity. This same power becomes our own as catechists when we choose to love our students with that same divinely inspired passion that is Jeremiah's greatest gift.

For Thought and Discussion

1. Are you passionate about your ministry as a catechist? How do you experience this? How do your students experience it?

2. Talk about "covenant" with your class. What does it mean to them to say that they love someone unconditionally?

3. Do their images of God reflect Jeremiah's description of a God who loves passionately and without limits?

12

Miriam and Moses:
The Left and Right Hands of God

From the very beginning of Moses' life, his destiny was intertwined with that of his sister, Miriam. As the book of Exodus opens, we are told that the Pharaoh is trying to kill all of the newborn Hebrew boys in order to control the size of the population of Hebrew slaves. After hiding her newborn baby boy for three months, Moses' mother makes a heart-breaking decision. She realizes that the only way to save the infant's life is by giving him away. "When she could hide him no longer she got a papyrus basket for him, and plastered it with bitumen and pitch; she put the child in it and placed it among the reeds on the bank of the river" (Exodus 2:3).

As desperate as this decision seems, it is also quite calculated. The infant's sister, Miriam, is sent out to follow the basket down the river at a distance "to see what would happen to him" (2:4). What happens is this—the Pharaoh's daughter who is bathing in the river sees the basket and the infant inside and "took pity on him." Thinking fast, Miriam seizes the opportunity: "Shall I go and get you a nurse from the Hebrew women to nurse the child for you?" she asks. When the woman agrees, Miriam runs to get her mother, thus saving her brother from death and her mother from heartbreak (2:5–10).

Action and Interpretation

The next time the pair is featured together is in chapters 14 and 15. This is the dramatic story of the escape of the Hebrew slaves from the Egyptians through God's parting of the "Sea of Reeds" (commonly translated as the Red Sea). It is Moses, trapped between a great body of water on one side and the oncoming Egyptian chariots and charioteers on the other, who is able to calm the panic among the people, who cry, "Was it because there were no graves in Egypt that you have taken us away to die in the wilderness?" Moses gets them to follow God's instructions and to head toward the sea while he raises his staff. The rest, of course, is history: "The waters returned and covered the chariots and the chariot drivers, the entire army of Pharaoh that had followed them into the sea; not one of them remained. But the Israelites walked on dry ground through the sea, the waters forming a wall for them on their right and on their left."

A very dramatic escape, but what did it all mean? It is Miriam, identified here as a "prophet" (Exodus 15:20) who expresses the meaning of the events with the help of the other women in song and "with tambourines and with dancing." As we have it in Exodus 15, this song is a hymn of praise that both interprets the events and expresses the great joy of the people: "the Lord is my strength and my might and he has become my salvation" (15:2).

Throughout Israel's history the role of the prophet was a very sacred one. It was through the words and actions of the holy women and men God called as prophets that the people could understand the meaning of what God was doing through the events of history and what God required of them. Without Miriam's song, Moses' actions would not be understood as God's salvific action on behalf of the people. (To avoid a too literal interpretation of events, it is important to remember that both chapters, the narrative of Exodus 14 and the song in Exodus 15, were written down in the book of Exodus many centuries after the events occurred.)

An Ambiguous Conclusion

Moses and Miriam appear together one more time, along with their brother Aaron, in an odd story found in the book of Numbers (12:1–16). According to the story, set during the time of the forty years of desert wanderings, Miriam and Aaron "spoke against Moses" because of a marriage he had entered into of which they did not approve. "Has the Lord spoken only through Moses? Has he not spoken through us also?" they ask.

God is not pleased. Yes, God says to Miriam and Aaron, I speak to prophets "in dreams" but to Moses, "I speak face to face—clearly, not in riddles; and he beholds the form of the LORD." Miriam the prophet and Aaron the priest are conduits of God's partial revelation to the people. Moses, however, has by this time become almost a symbol for the entire community. It is only within the whole people of God that God's ways can be fully known. Thus, Miriam and Aaron receive a lesson in humility.

What is not so clear is why only Miriam is punished with a week-long case of leprosy. That Aaron would be spared—especially given his own checkered past in serving God (see the story of the golden calf in Exodus 32)—is puzzling. Is it a way of indicating that, because of Miriam's great gift, more was expected of her? Or is it evidence of a bias against both women and prophets in a book whose final editing was likely done by members of the all-male Temple priesthood?

The answer to the question is not clear. What is certain is God's call of both Miriam and Moses as partners in leading the Hebrew people to freedom and to a new identity as the people of God.

For Thought and Discussion

1. Who are the women and men in your life who have helped you discover the meaning and purpose in your own life?

2. Moses represents the importance of charismatic leadership in a faith community. Aaron represents the importance of ritual and formal worship in the life of the community. Miriam represents the unpredictable movement of the Holy Spirit as she leads the community to a deeper understanding of God's ways. How are these three dimensions represented in the Church at this time? What are the conflicts among the three?

3. Have your learners read about other important women and men who have "teamed up" to do great things? You can start with the Bible: Joseph and Mary, Simeon and Anna, Priscilla and Aquila (Acts 18). What are some powerful teams from the world today?

PART III

Heroes and "Sheroes"
OF THE
NEW TESTAMENT

And so our story of inspiring saints continues...through the ministry of Jesus and beyond.

13

The Samaritan Woman:
"Coming Clean" Feels So Good

During the lenten season of my first year at Christ the King high school I was informed that all religion classes would meet in the auditorium on a designated Friday so that students might receive the sacrament of reconciliation. I was horrified when I realized this meant I would have to take my most unruly class of eleventh-graders downstairs and try to maintain a quiet and prayerful atmosphere during the service.

My initial skepticism was swiftly replaced by an overwhelming sense of God's presence when the day arrived and one after another of my most hardened students mustered up the courage to go to confession and then quietly spent time in prayer.

Invited by Love

There's something about "coming clean"—when it's invited by love—that is incredibly freeing. It's a lesson we see in action as an unnamed Samaritan woman has a sacred encounter with Jesus. As Jesus gently invites her to come clean, she finds herself among those who have allowed the Messiah to free them from the limitations imposed by the practical necessities of human life.

The story of the Samaritan woman's encounter with Jesus is in John 4:4–41. She is on her way to get water in the town of Sychar in the region of Samaria when she sees a man sitting at the well who asks her for a drink. The woman is justly taken aback; it was a social taboo for a stranger to address an unescorted woman in this ancient Middle Eastern society. Even more astounding is that Jesus, a Jew, would make any kind of friendly overtures to a Samaritan.

Samaria was sandwiched between Judea to the south, where Jerusalem was located, and The Galilee to the north. The Galilee was also a Jewish stronghold. The Samaritans were the descendants of the ten northern tribes of Israel who had been conquered and all but obliterated by pagan invaders over seven centuries before. As a result, Samaritan culture was a rich mix of Jewish and pagan influences, something that their southern neighbors found abhorrent. For many of Jesus' contemporaries, even setting foot on Samaritan soil was to be avoided at all costs.

When Jesus responds to the woman's concerns by offering to give her the "living water" of eternal life, she accepts. Or at least she thinks she does. "Sir, give me this water," she says, "so that I may not be thirsty or have to keep coming here to draw water." She is genuinely open to God; the very fact that she engages Jesus in conversation proves this. She is, however, dutifully going about the tasks any responsible woman of her time must do and she is not yet ready to see that the very essence of what she has been searching for stands right in front of her. Encased in the practical considerations of her life, she can conceive of no other way to understand Jesus' words than this most basic one.

A Real Turning Point

The turning point in the story comes in verses 16 and 17. After the woman denies that she has a husband in response to Jesus' desire to meet him, she is forced to come clean. "You are right in saying, 'I do not have a husband,'" Jesus says, "For you have had five husbands, and the one you have now is not your husband." Jesus does not condemn her for her lifestyle. In fact, given the many ways women were economically, politically, and socially bound to their husbands in this society, the woman's way of life might be understood as a statement of independence. But Jesus does insist on absolute authenticity and integrity between words and actions.

Having been called by Jesus to be more authentic, the woman responds with a series of questions that reflect her lifelong quest for truth. The dialogue in verses 19–26 focuses on questions about who God really is and what genuine worship of God means. Gradually the woman's enlightenment leads her to the ultimate revelation of Jesus as divine Messiah. Exuberant, she leaves the well to return to town and to tell anyone who will listen of her discovery. Her water jar is left aside, and with it all of the practical considerations of her life. This woman becomes the first apostle to the Samaritan people. As the story closes, the people proclaim Jesus as "the savior of the world."

A Challenge to Catechists

The Samaritan woman's dogged determination to know Jesus and to understand his teaching can serve as a challenge for those of us who are catechists. We are called by Jesus to go beyond a limited and static understanding of religious education and to look at our students and our mission in exciting new ways. Each time we choose to respond to the genuine needs and questions our students present to us, especially when this is difficult to do, we are responding to Jesus' call to become more authentic.

By really entering into relationships with our students, as the Samaritan woman did with Jesus, we make the lessons we are teaching and the day-to-day ways we are living more truly proclamations of the gospel. Rather than seeing our students as empty vessels, we gather with them and with Jesus around the well and share with one another the "living water."

For Thought and Discussion

1. Place yourself at the well with Jesus. How do you picture him? What questions do you have for him? What questions does he have for you? Perhaps you could make this meditation a part of a prayer service with those you teach sometime soon.

2. Has there been a time this year when a student, a parent, or a colleague challenged you with questions as the woman at the well challenged Jesus? How did you respond? Are you satisfied with your response? Why or why not?

3. How have your students challenged you to look at the ways you think about and live out your faith? Do they ever ask questions that inspire you to do and to learn more?

14

Mary Magdalene:
The Heart and Soul of Easter

Sometimes I wish we could celebrate Easter in September. I'm at my freshest and I'm filled with the energy and enthusiasm I need to explore this most sacred Christian feast with my classes. By the time April arrives, the ups and downs of a normal school year leave me feeling a bit taxed at the very time I want to lead the celebration of the Easter mystery.

If you've ever felt this way, or if you are looking for a path less traveled into the heart of the resurrection, then consider the story of Mary Magdalene and her encounter with the risen Christ. The limitations affecting the life of Mary Magdalene are unique. Unlike the other biblical figures featured in this book, Mary exists on the margins of Scripture. Nothing is known about her life except a hard-to-understand phrase in the appendix of Mark's gospel that identifies her as the one "from whom he [Jesus] cast out seven demons" (Mark 16:9).

The tradition in the Church that identifies Mary Magdalene as a repentant prostitute was formulated centuries after the gospels were written. Unlike Peter and other followers of Jesus, she is never featured in the course of Jesus' ministry. It is Mary, however, who is present at the crucifixion and at the empty tomb that first Easter morning, according to all four gospels. Clearly much of the story remains untold.

Mary at the Tomb

The most beautiful of all the resurrection stories involving Mary is found in chapter 20 of the Gospel of John. Seeing that the stone that sealed Jesus' tomb had been rolled away when she visits early Sunday morning, Mary fears that the body of Jesus has been stolen. She hurries back to tell Peter and "the other disciple whom Jesus loved." After the two men inspect the tomb and return home (Peter in confusion and the unnamed disciple with faith), a weeping Mary remains behind. What happens next astounds her.

Mary looks down into the tomb herself. (Entrance into the type of rock-hewn tomb described in the Passion accounts required the visitor to walk down a few steps after passing through a small vestibule just inside the tomb opening). She sees two angels who ask her why she is crying. After she expresses her fear that Jesus' body has been stolen, she turns around to see a man she assumes to be the caretaker.

She pleads with him to tell her where Jesus' body has been taken, but when the man addresses her by name she realizes that her plea will go unanswered. There is no dead body to be found because the man standing before her she now recognizes is Jesus. The Messiah—Christ, in Greek—whom her people have so long and so fervently waited for, stands before her!

She Is Transformed

This personal encounter with the risen Jesus transforms Mary's perceptions of reality. What she thought was the final indignity of grave desecration, discovered at the place where her hopes had been buried, she now sees as a sign of eternal life. The light that is dawning on this first Easter morning is not only the light of a new day but of a new era in which God and human beings will never be separated from one another or limited by death. Mary's meeting with the risen Jesus at the empty tomb is a dramatic interpretation of the fundamental resurrection experience for any believer.

We encounter the risen Christ most clearly in those moments when we are brought to see that our deepest experiences of despair and absence are really the abiding presence of God in disguise. In those moments we, too, become aware that our hopes and dreams are not dead. It is our concepts of happiness, which were too little to contain all of the joy God intends for us, that have passed away.

Mary would like nothing better at this point in the story than to hold Jesus close and bask in the euphoria of the moment. But Jesus has work for her to do. "Do not continue to hold on to me," Jesus says, "But go to my brothers and tell them, I am going to my Father and your Father, to my God and your God." Mary goes forth as the first to proclaim the joyful news at the heart of the gospels: "I have seen the Lord." Jesus is Messiah because Jesus is God. And God is with us.

Mary Disappears

As Mary goes forth with her proclamation, she disappears from the Scriptures. What happens to her after the events depicted in John can only be the subject of conjecture. Clearly the early Church treasured her witness, however, because the gospel that contains this story was written many years after Mary's death. To this day the Church continues to honor Mary as a saint. Her most enduring legacy for all of us who are her spiritual descendants may well be the model she offers of genuine discipleship. In the midst of her grief and fear, Mary holds on to a faith that is even deeper and finds it to be the means by which she can encounter the risen Christ.

So perhaps it's not bad timing after all that we have to wait late into the school year to help our students understand some of what the resurrection means. Just as Mary had to walk with Jesus awhile to discover the resurrection, so we must show our students our love and concern for them and our own commitment to the faith we proclaim before our words can have any real meaning. And then as we set them off to proclaim the gospel message in the varied ways God calls them to do so, we stand with Mary and the divine caretaker, knowing that those we teach never have to journey alone.

For Thought and Discussion

1. Reflect on a time in your life when a situation that seemed hopeless turned out to have a happy ending or a time when what seemed to be an unsustainable burden turned out to be a moment of grace. Invite your youngsters to do the same reflection.

2. Imagine that you are Mary Magdalene in the story. When you look into that empty tomb, what do you see? How do you feel? What is the moment like when you recognize that the other figure in the garden is Jesus? What does he look like?

3. Write the word "Resurrection" on the board for your students. Read the story in John 20 about Jesus and Mary Magdalene. Invite the youngsters to offer a word or phrase that summarizes what resurrection means to them.

4. With your students, write the biography of Mary Magdalene. What happened to her after this story?

15

Mary: *Saying "Yes" Was Only the Beginning*

Being a disciple of Jesus means being a "Yes man"—or woman, as the case may be. We begin to do the work God has called us to do the moment we make a decision of the will to respond to the promptings of the Holy Spirit within us.

The "Yes" that Mary speaks opens the way for salvation history to reach its fulfillment. While popular conceptions of Mary conjure up images of a queen who shares the glory and majesty of eternal life at the right hand of her Son, a closer look at the story of the Annunciation presented in the gospel of Luke reveals an awestruck young girl left alone to ponder the inscrutable holiness of God.

As the account of the Annunciation (Luke 1:26–38) opens, the angel Gabriel greets Mary with a profound message, "Hail, favored one! The Lord is with you." No details about Mary's background are given except that she is betrothed to Joseph. The betrothal was the time of preparation after a contract of marriage was agreed upon by the fathers of the bride and groom and generally lasted about a year. It was common for girls in Jesus' society to become betrothed after the onset of puberty, so it's not surprising that this child on the verge of womanhood is "greatly troubled" upon hearing Gabriel's words.

Presumably in an effort to comfort her, the angel tells her not to be afraid and reminds her again that she has found favor with God. Just how much so is revealed in the next bit of astounding news: "Behold, you will conceive in your womb and bear a son, and you shall name him Jesus." Gabriel's description of this special child draws heavily on the promise God makes to King David in 2 Samuel 7, a promise that was understood by Jesus' Jewish contemporaries as a Messianic prophesy. Mary, then, is about to become the unwed mother of the Messiah!

The question Mary asks next offers us a glimpse into her profound faith life. Having enjoyed the intimacy with God that goes with living in Covenant, Mary has the confidence to approach God, through Gabriel, with her most immediate concern. "How can this be, since I have no relations with a man?"

Gabriel says, "The Holy Spirit will come upon you, and the power of the Most High will overshadow you. Therefore the child to be born will be called holy, the Son of God." While it's not easy to know what significance such a title would have for Mary, by the time Luke is writing his gospel, toward the end of the first century, the title Son of God is a clear designation of Jesus' divinity. First Messiah, and now Son of God.

The further we choose to enter into relationship with God the further the mystery deepens. Mary has now entered so far into the particular mystery of the incarnation that she must either surrender to it or reject it totally. When Mary says, " May it be done to me according to your word" she gives the "Yes" that allows her womb and through her all of the world to become impregnated with the seed of a New Creation. Such faith does God have in humanity that the Omnipotent Creator of the Universe allows salvation history to depend on the "Yes" of a teen-age girl. Such faith does Mary have in God that she confidently heads into an uncertain future supported only by God's promise.

This profound encounter with the sacred ends simply: "Then the angel departed from her." Though Mary will appear sporadically in the gospel traditions, she will never be presented in such a profound encounter with God again. Her "Yes" will take her into the darkest kind of night imaginable as she sees her child brutally murdered. But the faith and love that enabled Mary to speak that "Yes" will also carry her through the darkness into the dawn of hope that we call the resurrection. In that glorious moment, one that must have infused the rest of Mary's life with an almost incomprehensible joy, she discovers that her "Yes" to God has been the reflection of God's "Yes" to humanity's pleas for deliverance and forgiveness.

Through our ministry as catechists, God will entrust to us some of his precious children and ask us to do our best to care for them and share with them our experience of the unconditional love that sustains the universe. Mary's story reminds us that our "Yes" allows Jesus into our classrooms just as surely as her answer allowed the Son to enter into creation.

For Thought and Discussion

1. Reflect on the ways you have said "Yes" to God in your life. When has this "Yes" been most difficult? Why? How has your life been changed?

2. What questions do you have for God? How does God respond in prayer? Where in your life right now are you being called simply to trust?

3. A well-known prayer that follows just after the story of the Annunciation is the Magnificat (Luke 1:46–55). Read it with your youngsters and ask them to write their own "thank you" prayers to God. (You might want to discuss with older students some of the social justice implications of such verses as 51–53)

4. Find some reproductions of artistic representations of the Annunciation throughout history. Have your students read the account in Luke's gospel and draw their own images of the encounter.

16

Joseph:
"To Dream the Impossible Dream"

Joseph, the foster father of Jesus, has been a fixture of popular Catholic art for centuries. It is easy to imagine him in the carpentry shop, the young Jesus at his side, or standing next to Mary as she cradles the infant Jesus at his birth. Yet Joseph is one of the most enigmatic figures in the New Testament; outside of the Infancy Narrative in the Gospel of Matthew, there are practically no traces of him. Joseph's virtual absence in the rest of the gospel tradition stands in sharp contrast to the series of intense encounters Joseph has with God through dreams as depicted in the first two chapters of Matthew. It appears that Joseph's "Yes" to God—a call to be the father of Jesus and husband of Mary—means sacrificing his place as the center of his own domestic universe in the patriarchal society of his time.

According to Matthew's gospel, the turning point in Joseph's life plays itself out over the course of four separate dreams. The opening verses of the birth story of Jesus find Joseph facing a serious dilemma: the woman to whom he has been betrothed is pregnant (Matthew 1:18–19). Knowing that he is not the father—Mathew explicitly states that Mary is "with child from the Holy Spirit"—Joseph plans to divorce Mary quietly and allow her to go her own way. According to the marriage customs and laws of the time, betrothal—the formal time of preparation before a marriage—had the same legal binding effect as marriage. Knowing that he is not the father's child, Joseph realizes that once Mary is found to be with child she risks death by stoning—the penalty at the time for adultery. The only way that Joseph can prevent this is by signing a legal document saying that he is divorcing Mary and reimbursing Mary's family for whatever dowry he might have received. Being a "righteous man," this is what Joseph is planning to do.

Things change dramatically, though, when "an angel of the Lord" appears to Joseph in a dream, explains why Mary is pregnant, and tells Joseph about Jesus' mission. Upon waking, Joseph, "did as the angel of the Lord commanded him; he took her as his wife." In so doing, Joseph runs the risk of being considered a cuckold—a husband whose wife has committed adultery against him—probably the most vicious charge against a man's virility in this patriarchal society.

But the upheaval in Joseph's life does not stop here. In the second of his dream encounters, Joseph is instructed to leave Bethlehem, the family's hometown according to Matthew's gospel, and head for Egypt to escape the wrath of King Herod (Matthew 2:13–15). Again Joseph obeys without hesitation, even though this will mean taking on the role of a rootless immigrant in a foreign land. For the sake of the welfare of the Holy Family and thus all of human salvation, Joseph has to sacrifice the very things that embody the good life in the ancient world—ancestral land-holdings and biological descendents. The very things, in fact, that God promised to Abraham at the initiation of the Covenant.

The final two brief dream encounters serve the purpose of explaining why Mary, Joseph, and Jesus return to Israel (Herod is dead), but not to Bethlehem (Herod's son is worse). Instead, they find their way into the territory of a more benign ruler in the north, settling in the region of The Galilee, in the town of Nazareth (2:19–23). Except for a brief mention in Luke when Jesus is twelve years old, this is the last time we will meet Joseph in any of the gospels.

Joseph's presence continues to be felt, however. Joseph's openness to a calling from God that he doesn't fully understand continues in his foster child's struggles to come to terms with his own mission. Jesus must follow it where it leads even when that means surrendering the approval of "good" people and finding himself surrounded by sinners. We see Joseph's willingness to let go of the rights and privileges of his status in life continue in his foster child's refusal to accept worldly acclaim or riches. And we see Joseph's willingness to empty himself for the sake of his family magnified infinitely in Jesus' willingness to empty himself for the sake of the human family on the cross.

It has been written that the goal of a good teacher is to make himself or herself obsolete. As we create an environment for our students where their nascent faith relationship with Jesus can develop and grow, gradually we lead them to a point where our intervention is no longer needed. When it seems as if the price we pay to be a good teacher demands too much from our own need to feel important, Joseph's model of spirituality can really help. If Joseph appears to move out of the center of the stories about the Holy Family, it is only because he has become the protective wall around its perimeter.

For Thought and Discussion

1. Spend some time thinking about and doing some research on the virtue of humility. Ask your students to share their thoughts or to give examples of what humility means.

2. What is the greatest sacrifice you have made or risk you have taken for the sake of the gospel? What particular grace do you need at this time to bolster your commitment to discipleship?

3. With your youngsters, create imaginary scenes from the life and times of the holy family. What events particularly stand out for your youngsters?

17

Simeon and Anna:
Waiting Upon the Lord

At first glance the "Yes" that Simeon and Anna give to God's call seems markedly different from that of Mary and Joseph. It appears that Mary and Joseph receive their life-altering calls from God when they are young. Simeon and Anna have almost lived out the sum of their days when God breaks into their traditional Jewish existence in a profound way. On closer inspection, however, it becomes clear that Simeon and Anna have said "Yes" to God years before. It is a lifetime of openness to God's will that prepares them for their sacred encounter with Jesus.

The story of Simeon and Anna (Luke 2:22–38) parallels the story of Zechariah and Elizabeth, the parents of John the Baptist, featured in the first chapter of Luke's gospel. Both pairs are older, both represent the established Judaism of Jesus' day, and the key events in the lives of both center around the Temple. The Temple plays such a prominent role in these stories because the building itself and the courtyards that surrounded it represented the essence of ancient Judaism. The innermost chamber of the Temple building itself, the "Holy of Holies," was separated from the build-ing's vestibule by a large curtain. Literally, it was the house of God.

Unlike Zechariah and Elizabeth, however, Simeon and Anna are not married. It doesn't seem as if they even know each other. Simeon is very much in tune with the promptings of the Holy Spirit, as are all of the "righteous and devout" characters in Luke's gospel and in the Acts of the Apostles. Luke says that "the Holy Spirit was upon" Simeon and that the Holy Spirit had assured Simeon that he would not die before seeing the Messiah. In fact, it's because of the Holy Spirit's promptings that Simeon is in the Temple courtyard when Mary and Joseph arrive with the child Jesus.

When Simeon sees the child he is overwhelmed with joy. "Now, Master, you may let your servant go in peace," he says, holding the child Jesus in his arms. Simeon is a faithful Jew awaiting, as his people had for centuries, the arrival of the One who was to save Israel. It is his openness to the Holy Spirit that enables him to recognize the arrival of a Messiah who will challenge his people's expectations.

As Luke will make clear throughout the rest of the gospel, this is a Messiah who will redeem through suffering. In the minds of most of Simeon's contemporaries, the Messiah would arrive as a conquering hero or perhaps as a prophet on a par with Moses. While Simeon is a believer in the same traditions, his openness to God enables him to penetrate further into their truths. In the midst of his joy, honesty compels him to share this insight with Mary: "Behold, this child is destined for the fall and rise of many in Israel, and to be a sign that will be contradicted."

The steadfast faithfulness implied in Simeon's life is made explicit in the description of Anna. She is called a "prophetess," a title indicating great respect for her closeness to God. (Deborah, the only female ruler described in the book of Judges, is likewise designated.) Anna is a widow who spends her days and nights in the Temple precincts in fasting and prayer. Given her brief time of marriage (seven years) and her advanced age (eighty-four) she might easily have spent several decades this way. She too recognizes whom the child Jesus really is, giving thanks to God on behalf of all who are "awaiting the redemption of Jerusalem."

In their devotion to the beliefs and traditions so central to ancient Judaism, Simeon and Anna represent the "Quiet of the Land" (anawim)—those who humbly remain open to God. Their "Yes" is essentially a willingness to cooperate with the Divine Will, never allowing impatience or their own pre-conceived notions of how God ought to work to compromise their ability to see God in the present moment. Simeon and Anna remind us of the importance of perseverance in our work as catechists. We always seek the presence of the Holy Spirit in our classes, asking God to help us move beyond our attempts to "figure out" our students and look toward the possibilities open to us in the present moment.

For Thought and Discussion

1. In your life at this time, how has the Holy Spirit been encouraging you to "wait upon the Lord"? What are the particular challenges you face in letting God's will unfold in your life?

2. When have you, like Simeon and Anna, seen God's working in your life or in the life of someone else in a particularly spectacular way? Describe the experience.

3. How have your experiences as a catechist matched your expectations of what it would be like? Where have you been disappointed? Where have you been surprised?

4. Ask your students to reflect on experiences they have had where God has appeared unexpectedly in the events of their lives or through the people they know. This could be done as part of a journaling activity or as a class sharing.

18

John the Baptist:
Prophet of Truth

Somewhere within the tapestry of our lives is the voice of Truth. For many it is embodied in a family member or friend or spouse. Others might experience it as the prompting of the conscience or the "gut feeling" or the still, small voice of God. For some it is all of the above. No one who is paying attention, however, can avoid those moments in which he or she is confronted by the stark realization that things aren't as they ought to be and changes need to be made. It takes a person of great courage, conviction, and compassion to be that voice that we so desperately need.

John the Baptist was such a voice. From his first appearance in the gospels—depicted as a "voice crying in the wilderness"—to his final days in a prison cell under the custody of King Herod, John bears an uncompromising witness to the Truth even at the expense of his own life. It is John's persistent clear-sightedness that enables him to be the first to recognize the uniqueness of the man from Nazareth at the very beginning of Jesus' ministry.

The earliest references to John the Baptist are in the birth stories of the gospel of Luke. The evangelist describes the wondrous encounter between the angel Gabriel and Zechariah, announcing that Zechariah's wife, Elizabeth, will conceive and give birth to a son, who will be named John (Luke 1:5–25). A second significant meeting takes place six months later between Elizabeth and her cousin Mary when the baby John within Elizabeth's womb "leaped for joy" at encountering the holy life within Mary's (Luke 1:39–45). It's not likely that either story has much actual history behind it, however. Most Catholic Bible scholars think that the stories developed long after the lives of Jesus and John as a way of expressing how important the Church believed John's ministry was in preparing the people of The Galilee—and perhaps Jesus himself—for the ministry, death, and resurrection of the Messiah.

John's story really begins at the Jordan River, where all four gospels present him performing a "baptism of repentance for the forgiveness of sins" on anyone who is willing to receive it (Mark 1:4). Coming out of the desert clothed in "camel's hair, with a leather belt around his waist" John is reminiscent of Elijah, the great Kingdom prophet of the Old Testament, as he announces the imminent arrival of the Kingdom of God (Matthew 3:2, 4). John is so focused on this imminent reality in which all human beings have renounced evil and opened themselves fully to the will of God that he has no tolerance for those whose response to his proclamation is lukewarm. When a number of the Jewish religious leaders of his time come to be baptized, they are greeted by words that sear through the façade of their piety and expose the hypocrisy beneath: "You brood of vipers!" John says, "Who warned you to flee from the coming wrath? Produce good fruit as evidence of your repentance" (Matthew 3:7–8).

Then one day Jesus arrives at the Jordan's bank. All of the gospels seem to have significantly reworked the historical core of this encounter between Jesus and John as the early Church struggled to explain why Jesus, who was conceived without sin, would need to receive a baptism of repentance. According to Matthew's account, Jesus insists that the baptism take place over John's protest. The reason: It is this baptism that signifies the anointing of Jesus as Son of God and thus inaugurates Jesus' ministry (Matthew 3:13–17). While the actual details of the encounter are probably impossible to reconstruct, the tradition as presented clearly reflects the high esteem in which Jesus held this prophetic ministry that preceded his own.

John's ministry and life come to an abrupt end when John's refusal to compromise the truth brings him into direct conflict with the political ruler of The Galilee, Herod Antipas. Herod's marriage to Herodias, the former wife of his half-brother, is unlawful according to Jewish law (Leviticus 18:16; 20:21), and John persists in his public denunciations of the marriage. John is locked away by Herod in a prison beneath one of the ruler's palaces. During the course of a banquet one evening the King is so delighted by his step-daughter's dancing that he promises to give to her anything that she wants. Prompted by her mother, she asks for "the head of John the Baptist" and thus traps Herod in an imprudent vow (Mark 6:17–29). The prophet of truth meets his end at the hands of a man who could not find the courage to renounce a foolish boast even though an innocent life was at stake.

The last words of John the Baptist as recorded in the Gospel of John provides what is perhaps the best insight of all into the true nature of this prophet. When some questions are raised concerning the possibility that Jesus might be usurping John's ministry,

John refuses to let his own pride get in the way of the truth. "He must increase," John replies, "I must decrease" (John 3:30). As catechists, how can we better honor this prophet than by rededicating ourselves to humbly performing the work of our ministry for the sake of our students?

For Thought and Discussion

1. With older classes, compare the story about the death of John the Baptist (Mark 6:17–29) with the Passion account in Mark's gospel. What similarities and differences do your students notice? (Another interesting project would be to compare and to contrast the accounts of the baptism of Jesus according to Matthew, Mark, and Luke.)

2. Younger children might enjoy illustrating the key events in the life of John the Baptist mentioned in this chapter. These drawings could then be combined to form a collage or perhaps bound together as a book. (Probably best to leave out the beheading.)

3. How are you doing as a prophet? Where are you being called in your life to bear witness to an unpopular truth? What are the greatest struggles you face? The greatest rewards? Is there someone in your life who is trying to help you face a difficult truth?

19

Martha and Mary:
Sisters in Faith

Although they are not always clearly identified, Mary, Martha, and their brother Lazarus figure in key moments in each of the gospels. The ways in which Martha and Mary interact with Jesus provide us with some valuable insights into the varied pathways leading to a deeper relationship with God.

Martha and Mary show their respect and affection for Jesus in markedly different ways in Luke's gospel (Luke 10:38–42). Shortly after Jesus begins his final journey to Jerusalem, he enters the village where Martha and Mary live. As Jesus makes himself comfortable in the house, Martha plays the role of hostess and busily carries out the tasks involved in waiting on Jesus. As Martha anxiously goes about her business, her sister Mary "sat beside the Lord at his feet listening to him speak."

Mary's Gift of Presence

Mary's actions annoy her sister who is "burdened with much serving." "Lord," Martha says, "do you not care that my sister has left me

77

by myself to do the serving? Tell her to help me." Jesus' response must have left Martha dumbfounded. "Martha, Martha, you are anxious and worried about many things," Jesus says. "There is need of only one thing. Mary has chosen the better part and it will not be taken from her."

There are times, Jesus seems to be suggesting, when simply being is much more important than doing. While both Martha and Mary truly want to welcome Jesus into their home, Mary's gift of her presence and her openness to what Jesus has to teach is the kind of reception Jesus yearns to receive. Martha's frenetic activity undercuts the very hospitality she so eagerly wants to provide.

Martha's Active Faith

Martha's more active way has its place too, however. As Jesus is on his way to Bethany where he will raise Lazarus from the dead, it is Martha who takes the initiative. Jesus hears of Lazarus' illness while he is in a deserted place across the Jordan River and makes a curious decision: He stays put for another two days (John 11:6). When he finally does head toward Bethany, Martha comes out to greet him at some distance from the town and wastes no time in getting to the point: "Lord, if you had been here, my brother would not have died." Given the context of the story, Mary's implication seems clear: "Where were you when we needed you?" Yet Martha is a woman of faith; having expressed her anguish, she now expresses her confidence in her friend: "[But] even now I know that whatever you ask of God, God will give you."

Martha's honest and faithful response to Jesus becomes the catalyst for a miracle. Your brother will rise, Jesus says, because, "I am the resurrection and the life." As Lazarus is brought forth from the tomb at the story's conclusion by Jesus' words, Martha's initiative motivated by her faith in Jesus is vindicated.

Both Authentic Disciples

The ways in which Mary's more passive way and Martha's more active way complement one another is most clearly seen in the story of Jesus' anointing. This poignant story, foreshadowing the impending suffering and death Jesus is destined to undergo, made such a deep impression upon the hearts of the faithful in the early church that some version of it can be found in the gospels of Mark (14:3–9), Matthew (26:6–13), and John (12:1– 8). While Martha is busily serving a dinner in Jesus' honor, Mary takes a jar of costly perfume, anoints the feet of Jesus, and dries them with her hair (John 12:1–8). Martha's actions are more numerous and complex, Mary's are more simple. Yet each sister in her own way responds in a deeply meaningful way to the presence of God.

Is one approach to God better than the other? The gospels offer us both Martha and Mary as examples of authentic discipleship. Modern Church history bears this out in the saintly lives of Thomas Merton—the contemplative—and Dorothy Day—the activist. As we make our way along the path that God places before each of us, Martha and Mary can help us be more attentive to those moments when Jesus calls us to the silence in which the Divine voice can be heard as well as the moments when we are called to work in partnership with the Holy Spirit to renew the face of the earth.

For Thought and Discussion

1. How well do you balance the active and passive approaches of Martha and Mary in your own ministry and life? How much time do you spend in the classroom leading your students in prayer and reflection? How much time do you spend actively involving them in the lesson? On a personal level, what are the opportunities for quiet reflection and prayer that you allow for yourself?

2. Ask your students to imagine that they will be entertaining Jesus for dinner that evening. Have them discuss the menu, the conversation, the entertainment, the guests, etc. (The imaginary dinner party could be portrayed by your students in prose or poetry, through artwork, or dramatic presentation, or even on film.)

3. In class read the story about the raising of Lazarus (John 11). Ask students to prayerfully imagine the scene as you slowly read it. What do they see? How do the main characters appear and act? After meditating on the scene, students could write about the experience or further develop the point of view of one of the characters.

20

Zacchaeus'
Change of Heart

Anyway you look at it, Zacchaeus is different. Among his Jewish contemporaries, Zacchaeus is set apart and despised because of his work as a tax collector. What distinguishes Zacchaeus most of all, however, is just how faithfully he takes Jesus at his word. His "Yes" to Jesus' invitation to come home will take him to absurd extremes as he goes about his act of genuine repentance.

Zacchaeus' story is found only in the gospel of Luke (Luke 19:1–10). No coincidence here: Luke often stresses the universality of the salvation Jesus brings. Time and time again, in the story of the Good Samaritan or of the Prodigal Son or here in the story of Zacchaeus, Luke presents to us a portrait of a Jesus who continually reaches out to those on the social, economic, political, and even moral margins of society.

Zacchaeus Goes Out on a Limb

As the story about Zacchaeus' encounter with Jesus opens, the town of Jericho is abuzz with the news that Jesus is on the way.

Jericho, located to the northeast of Jerusalem, is a major gateway to the Promised Land and is the last major settlement Jesus needs to pass through before he arrives in the environs of the holy city. Zacchaeus is eager to see Jesus but is faced with a real problem: A large crowd lines the streets, and he is too short to see anything from behind all of these people. The little man is determined, however; he finds a tall tree with branches that project out over the road, and he climbs it (Luke 19).

Climbing a tall tree—especially for an adult whose body has grown brittle—is always fraught with danger. But Zacchaeus has much more to worry about than this. He is a chief tax collector in the town, and that means he collaborates with the hated Romans who rule Israel in draining the population of whatever meager earnings they possess. (Tax collectors were notoriously corrupt, often charging exorbitant sums and keeping the excess for themselves.) As he sits there in plain sight on the branch, Zacchaeus is an easy target.

Jesus is impressed. Knowing full well who Zacchaeus is, Jesus looks up at the odd little man in the tree and calls out, "Zacchaeus, come down quickly, for today I must stay at your house." (I always picture Jesus smiling broadly as he says this.) Zacchaeus scrambles down and "received him [Jesus] with joy." In this sacred moment Zacchaeus makes a true act of repentance. "Behold, half of my possessions, Lord, I shall give to the poor," Zacchaeus says, "and if I have extorted anything from anyone I shall repay it four times over." (This was double the required penalty for robbery as outlined in Exodus 22:7) We are left to imagine the joy of the celebration that evening at Zacchaeus' house.

Sinner or Saved?

The crowd's reaction leaves nothing to the imagination, however. "When they all saw this, they began to grumble, saying, 'He has gone to stay at the house of a sinner.'" For Zacchaeus, the focus of this day was being in the presence of Jesus. For the others, the focus was their hatred of Zacchaeus. They allowed their bitterness to blot out any feelings of compassion toward the tax collector. By doing so, they miss the point of Jesus' visit and perhaps of his entire ministry. "For the Son of Man has come to seek and to save what was lost," Jesus says.

The story of Zacchaeus ends, then, with a tremendous irony. In the eyes of the crowd, the one among them who was farthest from redemption is the corrupt tax collector. In the eyes of Jesus, however, Zacchaeus is in fact the closest because he recognizes how far from God he has wandered and earnestly wishes to find his way back.

We might take Zacchaeus as an inspiration and work with the Holy Spirit to seek more clearly that one "lost sheep" within our classroom who needs our kindness and our help most of all.

For Thought and Discussion

1. With your class, reflect on the words of Jesus: "For the Son of Man has come to seek and to save what was lost." Who are "the lost" in our society most in need of experiencing Jesus' compassion and love? (Discuss as a group, create collages containing pictures cut from magazines or newspapers, or come up with a list to post on the classroom blackboard.) Conclude with a brief prayer service in which students will pray for "the lost" and

come up with one specific thing they can do to show Jesus' love and compassion to some particular person or group.

2. Reflect individually or in a small group setting with your colleagues on the following questions: Have you ever felt the joy of getting a second chance like Zacchaeus must have felt? Have you ever allowed your bitter feelings towards another person to "poison" your experience of God? (Try and be as specific as you can in dealing with each question.)

3. Who are the Zacchaeuses in your classroom—those who, for whatever reason, have become ostracized by the rest of the class (or by you?). Write a prayer for each of them. (You might give the student the prayer if you feel comfortable doing so.)

21

Peter:
From Darkness to Light

It's almost impossible to recall the story of the coming of the Holy Spirit and not think of Peter. According to the author of Luke-Acts, Peter, fearlessly and with great joy, proclaims the good news to the large crowd assembled in Jerusalem for the Jewish feast of Pentecost. "Therefore let the whole house of Israel know for certain that God has made both Lord and Messiah, this Jesus whom you crucified" (Acts 2:36). Can this be the same man who could not even admit that he knew Jesus? As we come to appreciate how far Peter's "Yes" to Jesus' call to discipleship takes him, we learn a lot about the way an authentic faith journey unfolds—both for Peter and for ourselves.

The man who would come to be known as Peter (his given name is Simon) first meets Jesus right smack in the middle of the busyness of daily life. One day as Peter and his brother Andrew are casting their fishing nets just off shore, Jesus beckons to them: "Come follow me, and I will make you fishers of men" (Mark 1:17). The very model of good disciples, Andrew and Simon leave their livelihood behind to follow the Master.

Peter's Act of Faith

In those heady, early days of ministry, Simon witnesses Jesus' meteoric rise to fame among the people of The Galilee. Awed by Jesus' miracles and impressed by his teachings, larger and larger crowds greet this teacher in each town he passes through. Along with many of his fellow Galileans, the fisherman begins to suspect that Jesus could be the Messiah he and his people have long been anticipating. Peter's chance to shine comes on the road to Caesarea Philippi when Jesus asks the question: "Who do people say that I am?" The disciples begin to make their reports, but then Jesus presses the issue: "But who do you say that I am?" Simon steps forward and speaks on behalf of the group: "You are the Messiah" (Mark 8:27 –29).

According to Matthew's gospel this is the moment when Jesus bestows on Simon his new name. "And so I say to you, you are Peter and upon this rock I will build my church" (Matthew 16:18). With this new title—a play on the word "petros" meaning "rock" in Greek—Jesus bestows on Simon Peter a new responsibility to be a disciple from whom others might draw strength and inspiration. To help Peter and all of the disciples understand what their commitment will require, Jesus begins to prepare them now for what lies ahead in Jerusalem.

Peter's Darkest Moment

The Rock promptly crumbles. "Then Peter took him aside and began to rebuke him, "God forbid, Lord! No such thing shall ever happen to you" (Matthew 16:22). A messiah who must suffer and die was not the kind of messiah Peter had in mind. Jesus' response cuts right to the heart of the tragic flaw in Peter's attempt at discipleship: "You are thinking not as God does, but as human beings do." Until Peter can follow Jesus unconditionally, his witness will never be the kind of foundation upon which the Church can be built.

It all changes for Peter on the saddest night of his life. His blustery pledge at supper on the night that Jesus is arrested (Mark 14:31) proves to be an empty promise. Shivering in the darkness outside of the building in which Jesus is on trial for his life, Peter fails repeatedly to muster up the courage to admit that he even knows Jesus. As the cock crows announcing the break of dawn, Peter is forced to confront the truth. In the most important endeavor of his life, he has been an abysmal failure. Now stripped of all illusions, the fisherman runs out deeper into the darkness and begins to weep bitterly (Mark 14:66–72).

A Second Chance

Christianity is the religion of second chances, however. In the glory of the resurrection experience, Peter comes to see that although he had betrayed Jesus, Jesus has not betrayed him. He receives the grace to enter into the dark nights of the future confident that the risen Christ is present in his own life and in the life of the Church. As Peter proclaims the good news about Jesus, following the promptings of the Holy Spirit on that first Pentecost, he has become the solid disciple Jesus always knew he could be.

There is much we have in common with Simon Peter. We have also been led to our ministry by a God who believes in us more than we believe in ourselves. We have been challenged to rethink our concepts of what our teaching ministry is really about. And the "Yes" we have spoken to God will surely bear fruit in the hearts and minds of our students far beyond our ability to comprehend.

For Thought and Discussion

1. Reflect on a "dark night of the soul" you have experienced in your ministry. What did you learn from it? Is there a sign of hope for the future that you can discern within it?

2. Re-enact Peter's denial of Jesus in the courtyard outside of the building where Jesus is on trial (Luke 22:54–62 is a particularly poignant version). Assign the parts of the different characters to children in your class. As an added twist, add a news reporter or crew to interview Peter and some of the other characters about the key events.

3. How open to the Holy Spirit have you been this year? Ask your students to write about a time when they felt the presence of God in a very clear and powerful way.

PART IV

The Parables of Jesus

Deciding on which of Jesus' parables to include in this section was not easy. From the point of view of the overall theme of the book— the power of Bible stories to transform us—it seemed obvious that the parables of the Good Samaritan, the Prodigal Son, and the Laborers in the Vineyard had to be included. Each of these stories challenges our categories of who is "good" and "bad" and what is "just" and "unjust" on the most fundamental levels.

Two other parables, that of the Fig Tree and the Dishonest Servant, grab our attention because at first glance Jesus seems to be promoting irrational or devious behavior. As for the Weeds and the Wheat and the brief Kingdom of God parables, the "metanoia" is not so immediate. Just as the leaven gradually makes the bread rise, however, so our experience of the Kingdom of God grows and grows as we allow these brief gems to settle into the recesses of our hearts.

22

The Good Samaritan

The parable of the Good Samaritan is found only in the gospel of Luke (Luke 10:29–37). Jesus uses this classic story of the Jewish traveler left for dead, the two distinguished representatives of Judaism who pass him by, and the Samaritan who cares for him as an illustration of how far God's call to love our neighbor can take us.

The Two Kingdoms

The reason for the Jewish antipathy towards Samaritans is rooted in history. Samaria and Judea, the two provinces immediately south of The Galilee where Jesus' ministry was centered, were the remnants of the Northern and Southern kingdoms of Israel in Old Testament times. According to the first book of Kings, the two parts of the united kingdom of Israel went their separate political ways after the reign of King Solomon in the tenth Century BC. About 200 years later the mighty Assyrian army conquered the Northern kingdom in 721 BC and sent many of its Jewish inhabitants into permanent exile. Over the next seven centuries these ruined northern lands, known by the name of their major city,

Samaria, developed a culture that liberally mixed Jewish and pagan beliefs and practices.

The "Faithful" South

The Jews in Jerusalem and the surrounding regions in the south viewed such intermingling with non-Jewish (i.e., Gentile) culture with horror. Through a stroke of luck in the form of the intercession of the powerful Persian Empire, the Jews of the southern kingdom survived their own exile in the lands of the Babylonian Empire (modern-day Iraq). After seventy years they were allowed to return to the Promised Land and rebuild their Temple and capital city. These returned exiles viewed with pride their ability to rebuild their sacred sites and to reinstitute the worship of their ancestors beginning in the late sixth century BC, while their northern neighbors had "sold out" to the pagans.

Who Is My Neighbor?

Jesus' decision to make a Samaritan the hero of his story turns the traditional Jewish understanding of "love thy neighbor" on its head. No Jew would ever have considered a Samaritan as "neighbor"; any enemies of the Jews would be enemies of God and thus excluded from consideration. The lesson of the parable is clear, however: In responding to the genuine need of his sworn enemy, the Samaritan has more successfully fulfilled this basic commandment of Judaism than either of the respectable Jewish characters.

There is another sharp irony in the story: The reason the priest and the Levite do not stop to help is because the man appears to be dead, and they are on their way to perform their sacred responsibilities in the Temple of Jerusalem. Jewish law required lengthy rituals of purification for anyone coming in contact with a dead body, purifications that would have prevented the pair from carrying out their duties. So while the pair follow the letter of the purity laws, they violate the spirit of the love commandment.

For Thought and Discussion

1. Who is the "good Samaritan" in your life? Who is the beaten traveler left for dead who needs your help now? In what ways does this parable challenge you to look at your life differently?

2. Share with your students some background information on the parable of the Good Samaritan. Have the class come up with a list of people they tend to look down upon the way the Jews of Jesus' time looked at the Samaritans. Finally, have them role play a "Samaritan situation" in which they have to decide whether or not they are going to help a person in need.

3. Read, talk about, or act out one of these children's stories, which can be linked with Jesus' teaching on compassion: From *The Book of Virtues* by William J. Bennett, "Old Mr. Rabbit's Thanksgiving Dinner," by Carolyn Bailey; "Grandmother's Table," adapted from the Grimm Brothers; "Tico and the Golden Wings," by Leo Lionni (Random House).

23

The Dishonest Steward

If they ever give out the Rodney Dangerfield "I Don't Get No Respect" Award for parables in the gospels, I will nominate this one (Luke 16:1–8). We expect that wickedness is to receive its just reward when Jesus begins the parable by saying, "A rich man had a steward who was reported to him for squandering his property. He summoned him and said, 'Prepare a full account of your stewardship, because you can no longer be my steward.'" Then Jesus throws us a curve.

The steward decides to ingratiate himself with his master's debtors by secretly meeting with them and by sharply reducing their debts. What is the master's response when he learns of his steward's latest scam? "And the master commended that dishonest steward for acting prudently," Jesus says. It's easy to see why Luke is quick to offer several previously unrelated teachings of Jesus to explain the point of the parable in verses 8–13. How could Jesus—the embodiment of truth and integrity—honor deceit?

A Lesson in Focusing

Jesus doesn't honor deceit. To understand why, look first at that charge made against the steward in verse one. According to the *New Jerome Biblical Commentary* (Luke, 155), the original Greek word translated as "reported" in English, implies that the accusation is a false one. It's also well known by scholars of the Bible that a system of usury—charging exorbitant interest on loans—was firmly in place in Palestine during Jesus' time despite prohibitions against such practices in the Hebrew Bible (Old Testament). When the "dishonest" steward starts slashing the amounts owed by the debtors, he's not cheating the rich man. He's eliminating the interest. (In one case, this reduces the debt from 100 measures of olive oil to 50!) Jesus' story, when properly understood, could well be one about an innocent man doing the best he can to survive within an unfair situation.

In his attempt to cope with a seemingly unavoidable fate, the steward does not allow himself to be consumed by feelings of self-pity or revenge. He focuses on getting himself out of his predicament and relentlessly pursues this mission using any means available. Jesus' final comments suggest there is a lesson in discipleship here: "For the children of this world are more prudent in dealing with their own generation than are the children of light."

All of us who have committed ourselves to discipleship understand the importance of the call to proclaim the gospel message. Do we pursue this mission with the same passion that the steward demonstrated in trying to save his own skin? Are we as resourceful and creative in searching for ways to discern the will of the Holy Spirit and to cooperate with it? Jesus challenges us in this parable to honestly look inward and see if our efforts to help in the building of the Kingdom of God measure up to the efforts we exert to protect our own self-interest.

For Thought and Discussion

1. Where in your life is the pull towards protecting and advancing your own interests stronger than the call to discipleship? Why? What needs to change?

2. There's a famous saying that goes: "If you were accused of the crime of being a Christian, would there be enough evidence to convict you?" Would there be?

3. Discuss examples of being honest and being dishonest with your students. Perhaps each child could illustrate one or two of their examples in the form of ornaments that could be hung on a "Truth Tree" in the front of the classroom. (You might even extend the exercise by creating a garbage dump into which children could throw symbols of the times they weren't so honest.)

4. Have the children think about a time when they were accused of something that they didn't do. How did they feel? What happened? Have they ever accused someone else falsely? Conclude by discussing why spreading gossip and rumors is so hurtful.

24

The Prodigal Son
—and Our Prodigal Father

Every American carries the picture around in his or her head. It's the picture of that first Thanksgiving Day, with Pilgrims and Native Americans assembled to enjoy the feast. Whatever the historical validity, the scene has a grip on our imaginations. It's a visual expression of our belief that in America people coming from different backgrounds can find common ground upon which to celebrate together. Such is the wish of the Father concerning his two sons in the parable of the Prodigal Son (Luke 15:11–32).

As the plot of this well-known parable unfolds, the younger of two sons commits a gross violation of the fourth Commandment. Unconcerned for his father's welfare in a time when children were in the labor force and Social Security did not exist, the son asks for his share of his inheritance. His father grants the request, and the younger son moves to a distant Gentile land, but soon he is broke and driven by near starvation to tend the pigs of a local farmer. How much worse can it get for a Jew than to be reduced to ruin amid the animals counted among the most abhorrent of all species in the Hebrew dietary laws? (See Leviticus 11:1–8, for example.)

A Lavish Welcome

When the younger son finally "comes to his senses" and returns home, he is overwhelmed by the welcome he receives. His father, who has been vigilantly watching for his son's return, rushes out to greet him. The son barely has time to speak before his father, "filled with compassion," showers him with the belongings proper to the son of a rich man and calls on his servants to prepare a great feast. This is the kind of abundant and unconditional love God is eager to bestow on each of us, most fully through the life and death and resurrection of Jesus. Do we experience God in this way? If so, our response could only be one of humble gratitude.

The Older Son's Fury

When the older son learns what has happened, he is furious with his father: "Look, all these years I served you and not once did I disobey your orders; yet you never gave me even a young goat to feast on with my friends. But when your son returns who swallowed up your property with prostitutes, for him you slaughter the fattened calf." Once again the father must reach out to a wayward son and try to make peace. "My son, you are here with me always; everything I have is yours. But now we must celebrate and rejoice, because your brother was dead and has come to life again; he was lost and has been found."

Jesus ends the parable here and leaves us to wonder whether or not the older son will accept his father's invitation. We can debate about the justification or lack of justification behind the older son's anger. We can imagine a number of endings to complete the story, some joyful, some tragic. One point seems clear, however: The father's joy cannot be complete unless both sons share in the celebration. Are we also willing to do the hard work of reconciling with our brothers and sisters and thus give to God the only "thank you" that God seeks?

For Thought and Discussion

1. How do you picture God? In what ways is the image of the father in this parable similar and different to your image of God?

2. What are some specific things you can do to help members of your class reconcile their differences with one another? How can you be a source of peace and reconciliation in the lives of your friends, family members, and colleagues? In your own life?

3. Place yourself in the shoes of the older son. What would you do at the end of the story? Imagine a dialogue you might have with your father and brother (or sister).

4. Give each student a blank piece of drawing paper with the words, "Thank you, God, for..." written on top. Each student should draw or describe someone and/or something they are thankful for on the paper. Ask each student to illustrate some quality about him or herself or something he or she is good at on the paper also.

5. Ask your students to think of a time when they were really sorry for things they did wrong and were forgiven. How did they feel? Are there people who are sorry whom they should forgive? Students can reflect on and discuss responses.

25

The "Kingdom of God" Parables

Often the key to genuine repentance lies not in the specific acts we do but in the change of heart that motivates these actions. As we noted earlier, in the original Greek of the gospels the word metanoia, usually translated to mean "repentance," literally refers to the changing of our mind (and heart!) after reflection. Jesus presents to us in Matthew's gospel (Matthew 13:31–33; 44–50) five simple parables that will permanently alter our view of how to recognize holiness in this world if we reflect upon them.

Brief and Vivid Images

In Jesus' time as in our own, people wondered what the afterlife was like. Often we may be tempted to think of heaven as a place apart from our daily existence and from all of the evil and pain that distorts the beauty of God's creation. Jesus and his Jewish contemporaries, however, thought this reality was very deeply connected to earthly life. The arrival of the "Kingdom of Heaven"—God's "Kingdom"—would be complete in that moment when the last vestiges of sin and evil were purged from creation by God through the chosen Messiah. The five brief parables in Matthew's gospel have all been crafted by Jesus to masterfully communicate in simple but vivid images a sense of both the radical change and continuity that mark the reality of the Kingdom of Heaven.

Jesus first compares the Kingdom of Heaven to a mustard seed—the smallest of seeds that will yield a plant in which "the birds of the sky come and dwell in its branches." Likewise, Jesus says, the Kingdom is like a tiny bit of yeast that when left to its own hidden workings will transform the entire pan of dough (Matthew 13:31–33). Jesus gives even briefer treatment to three other images: a treasure buried in a field, a pearl of great price, and a net brought out of the sea containing all manner of fish (verses 44–50).

A common thread uniting all of the images is a sense of irony. The mustard seed and the yeast are too small to be seen and yet each in its own way will transform the landscape. Many will pass by the pearl of great price and the buried treasure unknowingly, and yet the fortunes of the person who gives his or her all to take possession of one or the other will be permanently transformed for the better. As the fishing net rises from the depths of a seemingly quiet and lifeless stretch of water it will reveal that the water is in fact teeming with life.

Questions Raised

What are the hidden wonders that surround us? Where are the signs—very likely in the most unexpected places—of the Kingdom of Heaven breaking into our communal and personal lives? Do we sense the sacred in those "pearls of great price" whom we teach? Jesus challenges us to discard our worn-out concepts of heaven as a place of harps and clouds and to look more closely for the intimations of holiness within ourselves and our world. It is this transformation within our minds and hearts that is the first step in our calling, from God, to cooperate with the Holy Spirit in the transformation of creation.

For Thought and Discussion

1. Reflect on the "buried treasure" you have uncovered in your career as a catechist. What unexpected gifts, talents, and insights have you encountered in your students and in yourself. Be as specific as you can be.

2. Consider the unique personality of each of the unusual "fish" in your classroom net. Over the course of the year, write a note to each student praising him or her for one particular quality he or she possesses.

3. How do you imagine eternal life? Is it real to you or do you think of it more as wishful thinking? Why? What questions do you have?

4. Write out the word "heaven" on the blackboard. Ask students to give words and phrases to describe it. Discuss the pros and cons of each image. Then read the Kingdom parables with the class and discuss some possible meanings.

5. After having read and discussed Jesus' Kingdom parables, have the students write some of their own. Remind students that each parable must be brief and based on common everyday images. Students may want to work in groups on this project. Have each student explain why he or she chose a particular image.

26

The **Fig Tree**

Images of God are a double-edged sword. Picturing God as a merciful Father eagerly awaiting his son's return, or as a mother bird watching carefully over her young gives us some real insight into the nature of God. Sometimes, however, we form images of God that lead us into one of two extremes. We may come to see God either as The Mean Judge or as a kind of Great Marshmallow in the Sky—a being so permissive that good and evil cease to have any real meaning. Parables such as this one concerning a barren fig tree (Luke 13:6–9) can help us find a healthier balance.

Anatomy of a Parable

The evolution of this parable is interesting. Bible scholars generally believe that the earliest version of this story is found in the gospel of Mark (Mark 11:12–14). It is presented in the form of a narrative in which Jesus curses a fig tree for its barrenness even though "it was not the season for figs." Matthew leaves this detail out of his version of the story but keeps the tale basically intact (Matthew 21:18-20). The sober warning remains undiminished: Any follower of Jesus who does not "bear fruit" in the form of an authentic Christian life is doomed.

Luke takes the story from Mark and substantially transforms it. First, the story becomes a parable told by Jesus rather than a story about him. (It is possible that this was the story's original context—see the New Jerome Bible Commentary, p. 619, Sec. 71) More significantly, Luke tries to strike a more subtle balance by focusing on the compassion of God without sacrificing the importance of personal accountability.

According to the parable that Jesus tells, the owner of a fig tree calls his gardener (the vinedresser) to cut the tree down after he finds it barren of fruit for the third year in a row. In both Mark and Matthew's version of the story, Jesus curses the tree after finding it barren only once. An even greater act of mercy follows. The vinedresser intercedes on behalf of the tree: "Let it alone, sir, this year also, till I dig about it and put on manure. And if it bears fruit next year, well and good; but if not, you can cut it down."

A Lesson in Mercy and Justice

Luke does not alter the basic conflict in the story. By emphasizing the willingness of the owner and the vinedresser to give the tree every possible opportunity to bear fruit, however, Luke reminds us that God so passionately wants a relationship with every person that all attempts at reconciliation will be tried. The breadth of God's mercy was demonstrated in the life, death, and resurrection of God's Son.

Though God does not cut down trees, some trees may fall. The warning in Luke's version of the story remains as clear as it is in Mark and Matthew. If the tree does not respond to the vinedresser's care in the next year, then it is destined for destruction.

Just as some trees are too diseased to be saved, all of God's graces will amount to nothing if a person refuses to follow Jesus and thus allow his or her particular barrenness to be transformed into an abundance of grace and new life.

For Thought and Discussion

1. How has the loving presence of Christ borne fruit in your life? What positive changes have you noticed in your life? In the lives of those whom you love?

2. What "barrenness" in your life needs the grace of the Holy Spirit at this time? Why?

3. Prepare ahead of time a large outline of a fruit tree and cut-outs of individual pieces of fruit. Have each student draw or describe one good deed he or she has done recently. Paste or tape each drawing to the tree.

4. Discuss with your students: What are some of the signs of a Christian who is like a healthy fig tree? See if they can come up with other analogies that illustrate the difference between a genuine disciple of Jesus and a fraud.

27

The Persistent Widow

The words "with liberty and justice for all" at the end of the Pledge of Allegiance refer to a civil liberty we take for granted—the right to due process of the law if we are involved in a civil or criminal court case. No such right existed in the Galilean society Jesus knew. If a person was fortunate enough to receive a hearing in front of a judge, neither plaintiff nor defendant had any means of protesting an unjust verdict. Against this background Jesus tells the parable of a persistent widow who pleads her case before a judge who "neither feared God nor respected any human being" (Luke 18:1–8).

Further compounding the widow's difficulty is her status in the patriarchal society of the day. Women in Jesus' culture generally had little power and influence. The situation becomes even worse if the woman is a widow who has no male relative to stand up for her rights. How can this powerless widow possibly get a fair verdict from a judge devoid of any compassion?

The Power of the Powerless

Amazingly, she succeeds. Jesus takes us inside the mind of the beleaguered judge who ultimately does the right thing albeit for the wrong motives. Persistence pays off!

Luke says that Jesus told this parable "about the necessity for them (disciples) to pray always without becoming weary." Clearly Jesus is not saying that God will only grudgingly answer our prayers. It might sometimes seem like that from our perspective, however. We learn early and often in life that every prayer we offer is not necessarily answered in the way we anticipated. Sometimes it seems that our prayers have not been answered at all.

Meditating on the parable of the persistent widow can renew our flagging spirits in such times. God always listens, and God can always transform our apparently futile efforts into instruments of power. The Scriptures and our own life experience bear witness that God's best work is often done through the seemingly powerless people of the world, and in those very moments of our lives when we feel powerless against the force of evil. It would be well worth our while to remind ourselves and our students of the limitless power of this sacred communication with God.

For Thought and Discussion

1. How do you experience God in prayer? How comfortable are you talking about your own prayer experiences with others? With your students?

2. Get together with a group of catechists to share success stories in the classroom. What insights have you gained? What moments with the children stand out as special? When have you been amazed at the powerful change for the better you have witnessed in a child? (Post a big sign outside the door before you begin: "This is a no-complaining zone!")

3. Ask your young people to give you the name of a powerful person (real or fictional). Ask each child why they think the person is powerful. How is Jesus' power different? (Young children can draw pictures of powerful people or characters.)

28

The Weeds
and the Wheat

At first glance it would seem that the parable of the Weeds and the Wheat (Matthew 13:24–30) is a catechist's dream. After Jesus teaches the parable to "the crowds" he gives a detailed explanation of every important detail to his disciples (Matthew 13:36–43). It's a parable with an answer key!

Many Bible scholars agree, however, that while the parable itself is well grounded in the oral tradition leading back to Jesus, the explanation of the parable is something the writer of the gospel of Matthew cooked up himself. (See the *New Jerome Biblical Commentary* on Matthew, Sec. 88 and 91, for an example.) The effectiveness of a parable as a teaching tool hinges on the right combination of clarity and ambiguity.

Jesus often uses images and ideas that his audience would have easily understood but combines them in a way that is unexpected and often startling. To hear Jesus describe a Samaritan (the sworn enemy of the Jew) as "good," or a shepherd who abandons his entire flock to find one stray sheep, would certainly make Jesus' listeners wonder. Parables are meant to get under our skin, to prod us into stretching our minds and hearts so as to be able to see God and our neighbor in new ways.

The Landowner's Decision

In the case of this parable, the startling image is that of a landowner allowing weeds that have been sown among his crops to grow up along with the good seed until the time of harvest. And not just any weeds—the original Greek word refers to a poisonous weed that looks like the wheat it has presumably infested in the crop's early stages (See the footnote to Matthew 13:25 in the New American Bible.) As the landowner's workers provide nourishment for the wheat, therefore, they will inadvertently nourish the destructive weeds as well. What could the landowner be thinking?

The landowner recognizes that precisely because the weeds look so much like the good crop it would be impossible to root them out without destroying a good part of the wheat as well. The situation will be much different at harvest time when the wheat has reached its maturity. At that time, the landowner will say to his workers, "'First collect the weeds and tie them in bundles for burning; but gather the wheat into my barn." Patience and tolerance now will result in a greater abundance later.

Does it sometimes seem to you that God is incredibly tolerant toward the forces of evil? By allowing a comparison between God and the landowner in the story, the parable of the weeds and the wheat challenges us to turn our thinking around on this subject. Perhaps God's focus is not on what ought to be destroyed but rather on what can be saved. Just as the landowner will not neglect even one single grain of wheat, neither will God allow even the least of his people to be overcome by the forces of darkness.

For Thought and Discussion

1. What are the weeds and the wheat in your own life? What enables you to experience the presence of God in your life? What prevents you from a fuller experience of God's presence?

2. Where is God calling for you to be especially patient and tolerant within your ministry? In your relationship with a child? A colleague? The Church?

3. Prepare ahead of time a sheet of oak tag colored brown or green to symbolize a field and blank cutouts of plants or flowers. Have each youngster create a symbol of a good deed or a good quality they associate with being a Christian. Using glue or tape, "plant" each cutout in the field.

4. With older children, this parable might be a good opportunity to discuss why it sometimes seems that God allows bad things to happen to good people. After reading this parable with your youngsters, allow them to present their reasons for why they find this parable helpful or not helpful in trying to gain some insight into this question.

PART V

The Rest of the (New Testament) Story

As I was organizing the various sections of this book I noticed that while most of the New Testament pieces focused on the gospels, there were a few that reflected on other books of the New Testament. I grouped them together to serve as a sampling of the richness beyond the gospels in the other twenty-three books of the Christian Scriptures.

29

Acts of the Apostles:
Amazing Saint Stephen

For me, the kind of Pentecost experience depicted in the Acts of the Apostles (Chapter 2) happened on Ash Wednesday in 1983. During my college years I was certain I had put "Catholic stuff" behind me, dismissing most of it as either superstition or the ways in which various authority figures in my life kept me in line. It was no surprise that I had forgotten it was Ash Wednesday until I walked by my parish church in the middle of that afternoon and saw people coming in and going out.

What astounded me, however, was the realization that swept over me: This formal faith tradition that I had inherited was inextricably tied up with my genuine encounters with God in my life. Rejecting one would inevitably mean rejecting the other. I consider that moment the point at which the Christian faith ceased to be something I had inherited and began to be something to which I made a conscious commitment.

The Power of Commitment

The life and death of Stephen, the first Christian martyr, is a magnificent illustration of just what power the commitment born of the Holy Spirit can have. When we first meet Stephen in the Acts of the Apostles, he is limited by his status as an outsider. The core group in the early Christian community consisted of the Hebrew-speaking Jews of Jesus' homeland in the northern part of Palestine. Stephen is identified with the Hellenists, Greek-speaking Jewish Christians who were either not native to Palestine or who came from the more cosmopolitan urban areas of Palestine (including Jerusalem).

The opening verse of Acts 6 suggests that these Hellenists may have been treated as second-class citizens: "the Hellenists complained against the Hebrews because their widows were being neglected in the daily distribution [of food]." Stephen is selected along with six others to address this inequity through their ministry of service. The Greek word for servant, diakonos, is the origin of the word "deacon." Stephen's holiness is particularly noted and seemingly soon after his commissioning by the twelve apostles his ministry takes on a life of its own. Many "great wonders and signs" are attributed to Stephen, and his knowledge of the Scriptures and zealousness silence all those among the Jewish leadership who seek to debate with him (Acts 6:2–11).

The author of the Acts of the Apostles (the same person who wrote the gospel of Luke) intentionally parallels the last days of Stephen with those of Jesus. Stephen is brought to trial before the Sanhedrin (the Jewish governing body) on trumped-up charges made by false witnesses (v.12–14). When asked to speak in his own defense, he declines. Instead, he launches into a succinct overview of the covenantal history of the Jewish people from the time of Abraham, through Moses, on through the rise and fall of the kingdom of Israel.

Stephen's conclusion reflects the fundamental breach between Jews and Christians, which was about to become a chasm, as Luke writes in Acts of the Apostles: "You stiff-necked people, uncircumcised in heart and ears, you always oppose the Holy Spirit. You received the law as transmitted by angels but you did not observe it" (7:51, 53). From a Christian point of view, the Jews' focus on observing the exact letter of Scripture made them blind to its spirit—as embodied in Jesus of Nazareth.

The Result is Predictable

The end result for both Stephen and Jesus is predictable. Stephen is condemned to death for his blasphemous talk and is led outside the city to be stoned. As the large stones fall upon him, he dies, as Jesus does in Luke's gospel (Luke 23:34, 36), beseeching God to forgive his persecutors. When the story concludes by noting that Stephen "fell asleep," the author is not giving a euphemism for death but a bold proclamation of the Christian good news. The death that Stephen undergoes is only a transition to a fullness of life in Christ barely perceptible within the boundaries of the limited mortal lives we lead.

In an effort to convey the power of the Holy Spirit at the first Pentecost recounted in Acts 2, Luke uses the images of wind and fire, elemental forces of nature that dramatically alter the landscape. Stephen's story demonstrates how the "wind and fire" unleashed in our lives by that same Holy Spirit can utterly transform not just us but the lives of every child we teach. While living out the gospel message with conviction is both exhilarating and terrifying, when we do so we open our lives—and the lives of our students—to a richness and holiness beyond imagining.

For Thought and Discussion

1. Discuss with your classes some of the ways that Jesus may be calling them to be servants (diakoni) both right now and in the future. The story of Jesus washing the feet of the twelve apostles (John 13) might be a good Scripture reflection to tie in here.

2. Read *The Power and the Glory* by Graham Greene. Is the main character an example of a martyr? Why or why not? Which is more difficult: to die for what you believe in, or to live out your beliefs over a lifetime? Why?

3. Just before he is condemned to die, Stephen looks up and sees, "the heavens opened and the Son of Man standing at the right hand of God" (Acts 7:56). Using the footnotes provided in any modern translation of the Bible as a starting point, think about or discuss with others some ways this verse can be interpreted. How would you describe what Stephen sees?

4. If you teach older children, discuss the concept of "martyr" (Greek for "witness"). Can the students give examples of other famous women and men who have given up their lives for what they believe? Why do they think that the Church considers this willingness to sacrifice one's life for the faith such a powerful testimony?

30

Acts of the Apostles:
The Conversion of
Saint Paul

Saul of Tarsus' conversion experience on the road to Damascus reveals a most dramatic truth. The power of the risen Jesus to transform the world extends even into the deepest recesses of the human heart. It would be hard to find another person in Church history who has had an equally tremendous impact on the development of Christian belief and on the development of the Church itself—with the exception of Jesus! The letters of Saint Paul were the first part of the New Testament to be written and constitute almost half of the books that make up the Christian Scriptures.

Paul's Baptism

The Acts of the Apostles, written by Luke, tells us that Saul of Tarsus, a Jewish Pharisee, set out on a journey from Jerusalem to Damascus armed with an arrest warrant. He had the authority to take prisoner any Jews in Damascus he can find who have become members of a disturbing new sect known as the Way. This small but growing movement, which would eventually come to be called Christianity, held that a crucified prophet known as Jesus of Nazareth was the Messiah promised to Israel. The group's intense devotion to Jesus threatened to undermine some deeply held Jewish beliefs about the importance of the Hebrew Scriptures and of the Temple in Jerusalem.

As Saul neared Damascus, something extraordinary happened. "A light from the sky suddenly flashed around him. He fell to the ground and heard a voice saying to him, 'Saul, Saul, why are you persecuting me?' He said, 'Who are you, sir?' The reply came, 'I am Jesus, whom you are persecuting.'…'What am I to do, Lord? [Paul] asked" (Acts 9:3–5; 22:10).

With the help of his traveling companions the now sightless Paul was brought to a house in Damascus and baptized three days later by a Christian named Ananias. When Ananias laid his hands on Paul, "Immediately things like scales fell from his (Paul's) eyes and he regained his sight" (9:18). Paul was baptized, and according to his own words, spent some time in the Arabian desert trying to make sense of his new life (Galatians 1:17).

Paul Met Christ

What happened to Saul of Tarsus? Precise details are hard to nail down. Even within the book of Acts of the Apostles itself, the account of Paul's conversion is never described exactly the same way twice (22:3–16; 26:2–18). It's important to remember that Luke wrote the Acts of the Apostles long after Paul's death and probably fifty or sixty years after the conversion experience itself. What is certain is that Paul became convinced he had met the risen Christ in person on that day (see 1 Corinthians 15:8). He came to believe that the fulfillment of all God had promised to the people of Israel could be found in this risen Messiah.

Another certainty is that after his conversion Paul found himself to be a man without a homeland. Rejected by his Jewish friends and associates who saw him as a traitor and by the Jewish Christians who were suspicious of his motives, Paul went out to the far reaches of the Roman Empire making converts wherever he could. Paul's almost ceaseless travels would result in the same drastic transformation of the Church as had already occurred in his own heart.

For Thought and Discussion

1. Reflect for a few moments on the major turning points in your own spiritual journey. What are your most profound experiences of encountering God's presence? How have you been changed by these experiences? As far as you can tell, where is the Holy Spirit leading you at this time?

2. Have your youngsters read about and do presentations on other meetings with God recounted in the Scriptures. Some examples: Moses (Exodus 3); Gideon (Judges 6); Hannah (1 Samuel 1); Mary (Luke 1:26–38); Peter, James, and John (Mark 9:2–8); the Samaritan woman (John 4). They can then choose to do oral or written reports, drawings, short skits, and so on.

3. Challenge the children or teens to apply St. Paul's conversion experience to their own lives. Ask them to remember a time when they made a mistake and learned from it. Talk about how hard it must have been for Paul to make new friends after his conversion and to get people to trust him. Perhaps students can relate Paul's experience to their own adventures in making friends at school.

31

1 Thessalonians:
A New Life of Holiness

In this earliest written document of the New Testament, Paul must address the anxious questions of the local church in Thessalonica (located in Macedonia). Through his prayerful and thoughtful attempts to meet the challenge, Paul describes for us the essence of Christian living.

The Second Coming

The first generation disciples of Christ eagerly anticipated the second coming of the risen Lord. This belief was deeply grounded in the Judaism shared by virtually all of those first "Christians" and by Jesus of Nazareth himself. These Jews understood that the arrival of the Messiah (*Christos* in the Greek of the New Testament) would signify that the Day of the Lord had come into being. The Day marked the long-awaited time when Creation would be restored to the state of holiness described in the stories of Genesis 1 and 2. If the risen Christ was truly the Messiah, therefore, the righteous would soon be "snatched up" (in Latin *rapiemur* or, "rapture") by God.

By the time Paul writes to the Thessalonians twenty years after the death and resurrection of Jesus, many in that first apostolic generation have gone on to eternal life. Where is Jesus? The Christians in Thessalonica, who were being persecuted, were asking about the Day of the Lord, the day of holiness and salvation. What of those who had died in Christ?

Children of the Light

Paul is quick to reassure them: "For if we believe that Jesus died and rose, so too will God, through Jesus, bring with him those who have fallen asleep. Indeed, we tell you this, on the word of the Lord, that we who are alive, who are left until the coming of the Lord, will surely not precede those who have fallen asleep."

The reason? "For all of you are children of the light and children of the day." Paul will make this point more explicitly and completely in his reflections on the meaning of baptism in his letters to the Galatians and Romans, but already the divinely inspired idea seems to have taken root in his mind and heart. To become a disciple of Jesus is to become sanctified by God in the here and now! For the believer, death is not an ending but a transition into a fuller experience of holiness and life as a child of God.

Paul urged his brothers and sisters in the faith, who learned from him and the other apostles how they should live and please God, to do so more and more. "For this is the will of God, your sanctification." The believer is a new man or woman who has left behind a world darkened and limited by sin and death and entered a blessed world of limitless possibilities. When Paul writes that "we have not received the spirit of the world" (1 Corinthians 2:12), he means it.

Paul concludes with the comforting prayer, "may the God of peace himself sanctify you entirely; and may your spirit and soul and body be kept sound and blameless at the coming of our Lord Jesus Christ. The one who calls you is faithful and will do this" (1 Thessalonians 5:23–24).

For Thought and Discussion

1. What have been the moments of faith crisis in your life? How was your belief challenged? How was it strengthened? How did this experience change you?

2. Like Paul you are called to minister to the hopes, dreams, and fears of those whom the Lord has entrusted to your care. Spend some time during your sessions attempting to learn the hopes and dreams of your learners.

3. Write the word "holiness" on the board or post it in your room. Have learners brainstorm words or phrases that describe it. Who are some persons (past or present) whose lives have embodied holiness?

4. Implicit in Paul's idea of disciples united with Christ in life and death is the Catholic doctrine on the Communion of Saints. What does this belief mean to you? Have your older students do some research on this belief.

5. The belief in an immediate second coming ("Imminent Parousia") was the cause of a great faith crisis in the infant Church. What are some issues at the heart of the faith crisis in the Church today?

32

1 and 2 Timothy:
Building a Better Pastor

Saul of Tarsus, better known to us as Saint Paul, was a Jewish Pharisee who believed that the arrival of the Messiah would signal the end of the world as we know it. After Paul's encounter with the risen Jesus convinced him that the Messiah had arrived, Paul fervently sought to proclaim the good news to as many as possible before the final "Day of the Lord" came and God restored creation to its original state of perfection. Questions about how to organize and develop Christian communities in future generations were irrelevant.

Qualities of a Bishop

By the time Paul died—during Nero's persecution according to Church tradition—more and more Christians were coming to believe that the end of the world might not be so imminent after all. The so-called "pastoral letters" (including the letter to Titus as well as 1 and 2 Timothy) were likely written by the next generation of Paul's disciples whose churches sought guidance in choosing their leaders. (For the first several centuries of Christian history, bishops were customarily chosen by their congregations.) The letters were attributed to Paul himself, not through any intention to deceive but to indicate the influence he had on the anonymous letter writers and their communities.

The First and Second letters to Timothy, presumably written to one of Paul's younger fellow missionaries (see references in Philippians, for example), begin by listing the qualities to look for in a good bishop—such as self-control, hospitality, and gentleness—and in the deacons who would serve with him in ministry (1 Timothy 3:2–13; 4:4–9). The letters assumes both bishops and deacons will be married. The writer seems familiar with both women and men in the role of deacon. As to the most dangerous temptations leaders must guard against, 1 Timothy is quite clear: "For the love of money is the root of all evil, and some people in their desire for it have strayed from the faith and have pierced themselves with many pains" (1 Timothy 6:10).

Convenient or Inconvenient Preaching

In advising Timothy, Titus, and their fellow bishops on how to lead effectively, the letters exhort them to "pursue righteousness, devotion, faith, love, patience, and gentleness" in their own lives and in the life of the community (1 Timothy 6:11). A palpable spirit of mission formed by the Holy Spirit and grounded in the presence of the risen Christ must characterize all of the bishop's pastoral efforts: "Proclaim the word; be persistent whether it is convenient or inconvenient; convince, reprimand, encourage through all patience and teaching" (2 Timothy 4:2). Those cynics who reject the world as hopelessly corrupt need not apply: "For everything created by God is good and nothing is to be rejected when received with thanksgiving for it is made holy by the invocation of God in prayer" (1 Timothy 4:4).

Most important, in dealing with the inevitable questions and conflict that will arise, the leader is reminded to take on the mind of Christ, who "came into the world to save sinners" (1 Timothy 1:15). The people of God need their leaders to help them experience the love of God that flows into their hearts and into the heart of the community.

For Thought and Discussion

1. What are the most important responsibilities of a bishop in the Church today? Why?

2. Should bishops once again be elected by the faithful? Why or why not? What are the particular challenges that must be overcome for this method to be effective? What are some advantages of this method? (This could be a good topic of discussion for a teen youth group.)

3. Take your learners on a "cyber field trip" to the Web site of the United States Conference of Catholic bishops (www.usccb.org). Have your youngsters find information on the various committees within the Conference and about recent publications by the bishops. You might want to narrow the assignment to one particular aspect of the bishops' ministry—for example, on issues of war and peace or economic justice.

33

Revelation:
The New Jerusalem

The book of Revelation is the most misunderstood and misinterpreted book of the Bible. It's quite understandable why this is so; the symbolism contained in the book is so dense and sometimes so obscure that even scholars who have spent a lifetime studying the work are not sure what all of the symbols mean. In an attempt to make sense of them, interpreters often make a crucial error: because the author of the book identifies his work as a "prophecy," many assume that the symbols hide predictions of earthly events to come.

In fact, the focus of the book of Revelation is spiritual. Written during a time of intense persecution at the end of the first century, the book was written to bolster the faith of a Church that was beginning to question its longterm viability. Through a series of vivid images, sometimes beautiful, sometimes terrifying, the author proclaims the ultimate meaning of the gospel message. When all is said and done only the risen Christ, and those "washed in the blood of the Lamb" will remain standing. Evil and death will have been sent packing.

Jerusalem 2.0

One of the most inspiring tapestries of symbols comes toward the end of the book of Revelation. The forces of evil having been driven out by the Lamb (a common symbol for Jesus in the book), the author now sees, "a new heaven and a new earth." Having been purged of all wickedness and of all the effects of evil, Creation now appears in its full glory—an eternal glory within which death has no place. This is what we mean when we speak of "heaven"—not a separate place from Creation, but Creation itself purified and brought to completion.

At the center of this "new Creation" is a "new Jerusalem"—the city understood as the center of the world by the early Christians, who had strong Jewish roots. The city John sees coming down upon the earth is no mere human city, however, even a hallowed one. As the symbolic descriptions make clear, this is a totally spiritual Jerusalem, a city for all citizens of heaven—that is, all those who are in relationship with the risen Christ. Human words cannot fully express the beauty of this "beatific vision" as St. Paul calls it, but the author gives it his divinely inspired best. This new Jerusalem is as beautiful as "a bride adorned for her husband" (21:2). It possesses a "radiance like a very rare jewel" (21:11). There are twelve gates into the city—representing the twelve tribes of Israel—and the names of the twelve apostles are inscribed on the city's foundations. Both Gentile and Jew are welcome here.

In order to contain all of the children of God, the dimensions of the city are that of a perfect cube. Each wall is "144 cubits" long; that is 12 times 12—infinite dimensions able to embrace the "cloud of witnesses" that surround us now and which make up the heavenly community (21:12–17). The rainbow of colors described is simply riotous.

The Heart of Heaven

In the center of the earthly Jerusalem sat the Temple. In the bosom of the heavenly city, there is no need for a building, "for its temple is the Lord God the almighty and the Lamb" (21:22). It is the glory of the Trinity—God the Father, and the risen Christ, and the Holy Spirit—which the saints now behold directly, having no need for sacraments or ritual any longer. In the unimaginably bright light that emanates from the Trinity an angel shows the author "the river of life-giving water, sparkling like crystal, flowing from the throne of God and of the Lamb down the middle of its street" (22:1–2). This is the water of eternal life that Jesus promised the woman at the well (John 4), precious water that gives sustenance to "the tree of Life" that grows on either side of the river. What had been lost to humanity in the beginning (Genesis 3) is available to all God's children for eternity.

What is heaven like? These symbols suggest that the experience of eternal communion with God and with all of the saints—canonized or not—is marked by a heightening of our senses and a direct experience of God. The Light that will hold us in its embrace is Love, a Love that "will wipe away every tear." Truly we will understand the full meaning of the Incarnation then: "See the home of God is among mortals, he will dwell with them; they will be his people, and God himself will be with them" (Revelation 21:3).

For Thought and Discussion

1. What do you think that heaven is like? Ask your children to share—and perhaps—draw their images.

2. What are the most powerful experiences of peace, joy, and love in your life? How does it feel to think of them as glimpses of heaven?

3. What questions do these reflections raise for you? Hopes? Ask your learners the same questions.

PART VI

The Luminous Mysteries

OF THE ROSARY

The "Luminous Mysteries" of the rosary introduced by Pope John Paul II provide an opportunity not only to give a glimpse into the scriptural references behind the mysteries but to reinforce the connection between the rosary and the Scriptures. For several centuries, when most of the faithful in medieval Europe were illiterate, it was the rosary that offered the believer an opportunity to meditate on various stories of the New Testament any time he or she wished.

I'll also offer two brief reflections on scriptural accounts of the crucifixion and resurrection of Jesus as a way of situating the Luminous Mysteries into the broader picture of salvation history.

34

The Baptism of Jesus

The modern Catholic approach to Bible study and to the rosary each offer the faithful a way to a deeper relationship with the living Word of God.

The First Mystery of Light: The Baptism of Jesus

Christian baptism signifies the washing away of original sin and the beginning of a new life with Christ. What did Jesus' Jewish baptism mean? Also, what is the significance of the three things reported to have happened immediately after Jesus was baptized: "And just as he was coming up out of the water, he saw the heavens torn apart and the Spirit descending like a dove on him. And a voice came from heaven, 'You are my Son, the Beloved, with you I am well pleased'" (Mark 1:10–11)?

It was a common practice in Jesus' time for a Jew to totally immerse himself in water before worshiping at the Temple. This ritual had nothing directly to do with the forgiveness of sin, however. When John performs his baptism by immersing the willing in the Jordan River, he seems to have given the practice a new meaning: "He (John) went into all the region around the Jordan, proclaiming a baptism of repentance for the forgiveness of sin" (Luke 3:3).

Understanding the context of John's proclamation is crucial. As the rest of John's words in Luke make clear (3:4–14), he is anticipating the imminent end of the world as we know it and the arrival of the Kingdom of God. To accept John's baptism, then, is to show one's willingness to be purified of any obstacles separating the believer from God. It makes sense that Jesus of Nazareth, still growing in his understanding of his mission and his true identity, would have seen in John's call an opportunity to make a fuller commitment to God.

The Church's Understanding of Jesus' Baptism

When the evangelists set out to write the gospels several generations after the resurrection, their Spirit-given insight into Jesus' true nature as Messiah and Son of God inspired them to interpret his baptism in another way. They and the communities for which they wrote had come to see Jesus not just as a dedicated prophet announcing the coming of the Kingdom, but as the sign and instrument through whom God's Kingdom was established! To illustrate this insight, first Mark and then Matthew and Luke cloak Jesus' baptism in three powerful symbols.

For centuries the prophets had yearned for God to intervene in some direct way to cleanse the world of evil. As Jesus comes up from the water, God "tears open" the sky to signify that the day has finally arrived. The Holy Spirit, who descends in the form of a dove, connects this story to another in which God performs a spiritual renewal of the earth through water. In the tale of Noah's Ark (Genesis 6—9), it is a dove returning with a fresh olive branch in its mouth that provides Noah and his family with the first real sign that the re-creation of the world has begun. Jesus is also a sign of renewal, but on a much more magnificent level.

Just in case there might be any question in the reader's mind as to Jesus' divine identity, the evangelists describe God's voice calling down from heaven identifying Jesus as his beloved Son. When the three signs are taken together, the baptism of Jesus becomes a profound announcement that the spiritual destiny of the human race is about to be changed once and for all.

For Thought and Discussion

1. In what way is God calling you to radically change the way that you are doing things? Can you apply any of these insights to your ministry as a catechist?

2. John baptizes Jesus even though he does not fully understand why he must do so. Are there some commitments and obligations in which you have a difficult time finding meaning? Why?

3. Perhaps students could use this opportunity to do some research about their own baptisms. Do their parents or guardians remember any unusual events? What was happening in the world at the time?

4. Compare the three accounts of Jesus' baptism in Mark, Matthew, and Luke. What differences do you notice? Why do you think Matthew and Luke made the changes that they did? (A good Bible commentary will help here. Try the Collegeville or Sacra Pagina series, both available through the Liturgical Press).

5. Ask your youngsters to imagine that they were present at Jesus' baptism. Have them draw or write about what they experienced that day.

35

The Miracle at Cana

"Do whatever he tells you." With these words spoken to the head-waiter at the wedding feast in Cana, Mary expresses her faith in her son's ability and willingness to save two newlyweds from a socially disastrous situation. Yet even Mary must be overwhelmed by the abundance that flows—literally—from Jesus' response.

The miracle at Cana (John 2:1–11) in which Jesus turns water into wine is unique in the collection of gospel miracle stories. This is the only miracle that features Mary. It is the only miracle Jesus performs at a wedding. Finally, Jesus doesn't actually do or say anything that directly causes the miracle. All he does is direct some servants to fill six large stone jars with water. How can an understanding of the context behind this account, and of John's gospel in general, help us enter more deeply into the story?

The Wedding Feast

The setting of a wedding is very significant. Palestinian wedding feasts in Jesus' time could go on for days as visitors came and went. Wine was a staple of Jewish life and never more so than at festive celebrations. Given the great emphasis on hospitality in Middle

Eastern cultures both then and now, it would be imperative for the families involved to ensure that the wine never ran out. Mary, perhaps having been a victim of social stigma herself, knows what trouble these newlyweds will face if a dramatic turn of events does not occur immediately.

On a deeper level, John is using the image of a wedding feast to signify to the reader that something much greater is happening here than the miracle itself. The image of a great banquet or wedding feast is often used in the Hebrew Scriptures as a symbol of the Kingdom of God. (See Luke 14:16–24 or Matthew 25:1–13 for examples of where Jesus incorporates the same imagery in his own parables.) If the wedding feast is intended to make us think of God's Kingdom, then the bountiful wine represents the super-abundant grace of God to be poured out to all who, through Jesus, have accepted the invitation to take part in this greatest of all banquets. Just as there is more wine in those six jars than all of the wedding guests put together could ever consume, so there is more joy in God's Kingdom than we can ever imagine.

Jesus' Reaction to Mary's Petition

One more puzzling detail of the story deserves to be mentioned. While not unique (see Mark 7:24–30 for another example) it is unusual that Jesus initially refuses to perform the miracle. (See verse 4: "Woman, how does your concern affect me? My hour has not yet come.") This apparent refusal associated with the first miracle Jesus performs in John's gospel can also be seen in the last miracle Jesus performs in the same gospel—the raising of Lazarus from the dead (John 11). Upon hearing the news that his friend Lazarus is sick, Jesus remains where he is. He does not travel to Bethany until after his friend has died, prompting an implicit rebuke from Lazarus' sister Martha: "Lord, if you had been here, my brother would not have died" (John 11:21). What is Jesus waiting for?

The result of this last miracle is much more spectacular than what happens at Cana, but the parallel is important. In both situations Jesus is operating according to a plan known only to God. Likewise in both cases, the miracle that Jesus performs far exceeds both the request and the expectations of those who petition him.

Could John be suggesting in both these miracle stories that God's ways are often so hard to understand because God's gifts to us so greatly exceed the limits of our imaginations?

For Thought and Discussion

1. Do you believe it when St. Paul says that "eye has not seen, ear has not heard what God has ready for those who love him? " Have you had any life experiences that might reflect the truth of Paul's words?

2. Where are the six empty stone water jars in your life? Where are you finding difficulty holding on to hope and overcoming doubt? Have you asked Mary or Jesus for help lately? Write out your prayer of petition or lament.

3. Ask your children to imagine themselves as guests at the wedding feast in Cana while you slowly and prayerfully read the story. Children can write, sing, or draw pictures describing what they saw and how they felt.

4. Let your young people do a project on wedding customs around the world. Include in your study research on the wedding customs of Jesus' time.

36

Jesus and the
Kingdom of God

Over and over again, Jesus tries to open the hearts and minds of his listeners to the wonders of the Kingdom of God. The proclamation of the Kingdom is at the heart of every miracle Jesus performs. It is a vision that goes to the heart of who Jesus is. Precisely because of its all-consuming importance, however, the meaning of the concept can be difficult to put into simple words. Yet the joyous anticipation that is so much a part of a child's life offers us a great opportunity to help our students get in touch with the excitement contained within Jesus' core message.

The roots of a belief in the "Kingdom of God" run deep into the history of Jesus' Jewish heritage. For centuries after the establishment of their own kingdom, Jews fervently prayed for the arrival of the "Day of the Lord" when the grip of evil on the world would be broken once and for all and the unrighteous would disintegrate like weeds burned in a roaring fire. It is on this day that the reign of God would replace the reign of sin, death, and evil and return creation to the state of perfection God had always intended. The anticipation that God would break into creation in a dramatic way was given a new impetus by the collapse of the southern kingdom of Judah and the Babylonian Exile that followed in the sixth century BC.

Images of the Kingdom

There are any number of creative images depicting these events. See Isaiah 11:1–10 and Daniel 7 for two starkly different impressions of this particular cosmic regime change. Jesus continues the tradition of the prophets by incorporating equally vivid imagery in the Kingdom parables he tells. (Luke 14:16–24 and Mark 12:1–12 present two sharply contrasting examples.) Perhaps the most profound depictions of the quality of the Kingdom of God are the simplest ones found in Matthew 13.

Jesus presents images of a tiny mustard seed that grows into the largest of bushes, a speck of yeast that makes the mass of dough rise, a buried treasure revealed only accidentally to a fortunate farmer, a pearl of great price visible only to a trained eye, and a fishing net raised from the deep bursting with fish. All five parables are linked by a common thread: the Kingdom of God is already breaking into creation, visible to those with eyes of faith and hearts of compassion. And like the tiny seed, the speck of yeast, the almost indistinguishable pearl, the hidden treasure, and the unseen net full of fish, what the Kingdom will be like when it is fully established remains beyond our ability to comprehend.

Miracles: Signs of the Kingdom

Every miracle Jesus performs has a double meaning. While each healing is a cause for celebration on the part of the person who has been cured, the miracle also serves as a concrete sign of God's

Kingdom coming into being. Jesus says as much when John the Baptist's disciples ask him if he is the Messiah sent by God to usher in the Kingdom: "Go and tell John what you hear and see; the blind receive their sight, the lame walk, the lepers are cleansed, the deaf hear, the dead are raised, and the poor have good news brought to them" (Matthew 11:4–5).

With Jesus' death and resurrection, God's Kingdom is firmly established. The risen Christ invites his disciples to enter into a peace that has not been imposed from above by the powerful but that wells up like the waters of an underground stream when all human beings live in right relationship with one another, with all creation, and with God. Do we dare allow ourselves to live as if that is so?

For Thought and Discussion

1. How has your own understanding of "heaven" and eternal life grown since you were a child? What excites you? What troubles you? What unanswered questions do you have?

2. Reflect on the "Kingdom moments" in your own life. What experiences have you had that have revealed to you that you are called and destined to live joyfully? What have been your greatest temptations to despair?

3. You can use acorns for a modern illustration of Jesus' parable of the mustard seed. Pass some out to your youngsters and ask them this question: "If you'd never seen an oak tree in your life, would you believe that such a large tree could come from such a small seed?" Talk about other kinds of seeds; you might even

have the children plant their own flower or vegetable seeds and watch them grow.

4. Have your youngsters put together some sort of a collage containing pictures of people acting in ways that build the Kingdom of God. You can invite your students to explain why they chose the images they did.

37

The Transfiguration

Watch out for mountains when you read the books of the Bible. From Mt. Ararat in the book of Genesis to Mt. Sinai in Exodus to the unnamed mountain from which Jesus delivers his famous Sermon in the gospel of Matthew, the Scriptures are chock full of high-altitude divine encounters. When Jesus invites Peter, James, and John to travel up a mountain with him, it might have been wise for the three to pack their sunglasses.

Mark's Description

The story of the Transfiguration can be found in all three of the synoptic gospels (Mark, Matthew, and Luke). Mark's version, the earliest of the three, is set right in the middle of Jesus' Galilean ministry (Mark 9:2–8). Without warning Jesus is transfigured before the three apostles. (The actual Greek word is "metamorphosis.") There is no description of Jesus himself, but Mark does tell us that Jesus' clothing has taken on an intense whiteness—possibly a symbolic detail or perhaps a description of an immense burst of light. Conversing with Jesus are Moses and Elijah.

Summoning up the will to speak in the midst of his fear and trembling, Peter offers to build three dwellings so that the holy trio can stay and rest awhile. At that point this divine encounter reaches its dramatic climax as a voice from the cloud overshadowing the three men calls Jesus his beloved Son. When the apostles look up again there is only Jesus standing before them.

This explicit revelation of Jesus' divinity is loaded with meaning and food for thought. Jesus' two companions in dialogue are the two most significant human figures in the Hebrew Scriptures. Moses was the protector of and conduit for the Torah—the core beliefs and commandments of the Jewish faith. Elijah was the epitome of the Hebrew prophets who, through the centuries before Jesus, were called by God to interpret the Jewish Law for new generations of believers. In essence, then, Mark pictures the fullness of the Jewish faith in the persons of Moses and Elijah in conversation with the fullness of God's revelation in the person of Jesus.

An Actual Experience?

It is only natural for the three awed apostles to want to remain in this experience and try to understand it. The presence of Yahweh—God the Father in Christian terms—represented by the cloud and voice from heaven, makes it clear that this is not an experience that can be contained within the boundaries of time and space, however. It is important to notice that when the three apostles descend the mountain to return to the rigors, joys, and ambiguities of their lives, they do so in the company of Jesus.

Is the story of the Transfiguration a remembrance of an actual experience in the life of Jesus of Nazareth or is it a creation of the early Church inspired by the resurrection? Bible scholars continue to reflect upon that question. There is no question, however, that the story captures a basic Christian truth. For those who make up the Body of Christ any particular event in daily life is sacramental. Each seemingly ordinary moment in our lives offers us the opportunity to directly encounter God.

For Thought and Discussion

1. Spend some time reflecting on your own transcendent moments. Are any of them connected with your ministry of teaching? With your experience of Church? Where do you encounter the sacred most often in your life?

2. What are you trying to hold on to that you need to let go of? How aware are you of the real presence of Jesus in your life? Do your experiences of communal celebration of faith in your parish and in the larger Church help you in experiencing this presence? If yes, how. If not, why not?

3. Ask each of the children/teens to describe in detail a time when he or she felt particularly at peace or joyful or in awe. How does it feel to re-create that moment? Encourage students to express the experience through any means they want; writing, drawing, performance, or group sharing are all possibilities.

4. Have your children do some research on Moses and Elijah or on the significance of mountains in religion in general and the Hebrew Scriptures in particular.

5. Your youngsters can draw "before and after" pictures of the transfigured Jesus. Next, let them pretend to be Peter describing the events of the day to his friends.

38

The First Eucharist:
Celebrating God's Redemptive Love

The lenten season reaches its culmination by leading us into the events of the sacred Triduum—Holy Thursday evening, Good Friday, and Easter Sunday, including the great Easter Vigil celebration on Saturday night. Given the penitential nature of the season of Lent, we can become so caught up in the tragedy of Jesus of Nazareth's last earthly days that our experience of the profound joy located just beneath the surface of the events is compromised. The fifth Mystery of Light, in which we call to mind the full meaning of the Last Supper, can help us to focus more clearly on the total and complete gift of God's love that this season embodies.

Comparing the Gospels

According to Mark, Matthew, and Luke, Jesus and his disciples gather on that first Holy Thursday to celebrate the Jewish Passover feast together. When you compare the words that Jesus says over the bread and wine—the Words of Institution—in each of the three gospels, something interesting happens. The version in Matthew's gospel (Matthew 26:26–29) follows quite closely the version of Jesus' words in Mark's gospel (Mark 14:22–25). It is extremely probable that Mark's gospel was Matthew's source.

Luke's version of the words (Luke 22:19–20), however, are noticeably different. They more closely resemble the recollection of Jesus' words recorded by Paul in his first letter to the Corinthians (1 Corinthians 11:23–25). This seemingly minor difference in wording tells us something important about how sacred the memories and creative reflections surrounding Jesus' last meal with his friends were to the first Christians.

The existence of two distinct versions of Jesus' words at the Last Supper makes it unlikely that any writer is quoting the exact words that Jesus of Nazareth said. If such a memory existed, there would be only one version of Jesus' words. Why would any evangelist have changed them? It also is unlikely that each evangelist and St. Paul created the words from scratch. If they did, there would be more than two versions.

God's Ongoing Act of Love

The only explanation that makes sense is that even before Paul wrote his letters in the middle of the first century, and Mark wrote his gospel a generation later, the small Christian communities scattered throughout the Eastern Roman Empire celebrated a lively and somewhat varied re-enactment of the Last Supper. This first generation of believers searched for a way to express through liturgy the incomprehensible experience of God's love and forgiveness revealed in the resurrection. For this purpose they turned to Jesus' words and actions at the Last Supper. In their recollection of this first celebration of the Eucharist they came to understand that they were not only proclaiming an example of God's unconditional love from the past. They were also celebrating God's ongoing act of redemptive love through Jesus in their living communities.

The word "eucharist " itself comes from the Greek word *eucharistea*, which means "to give thanks." This is exactly what Jesus did before he broke the bread and proclaimed it to be his body and took the cup of wine and proclaimed it to be his blood and passed each around to be shared by all. The celebration of the Eucharist in our parishes today most clearly embodies Jesus' words and actions when, with hearts filled with joyful gratitude, we go forth from the assembly and share with others our time, our wealth, and, most importantly, ourselves.

For Thought and Discussion

1. Spend some time familiarizing yourself and your youngsters with the meaning and practices associated with the Jewish Passover meal Jesus and the disciples celebrated. Older children might enjoy reporting on the particular symbols and prayers that are part of a celebration of the Passover in a typical Jewish household today. Your class could put together a dramatic presentation of the events leading up to the escape from Egypt in Exodus 3—12. (A good modern retelling of the story that's child friendly for middle grade through high school students is Disney's *The Prince of Egypt.* Be prepared for some tough questions, though!)

2. Invite your youngsters to tell the class about mealtime customs in their homes. Are there any meals when everyone eats

together? Do they say grace before meals? What are some of their favorite foods and dinnertime stories? Any "theme" nights or special memories? Share your own experiences. Help them relate their personal experience to the community experience of sharing the Eucharist at Mass.

3. Take some time to reflect on the most meaningful meals you've been a part of in your life. Pause to relive them again in your mind. What made them so special? What blessings in your life are you particularly grateful for? Who do you need to thank?

39

From Darkness to Glory:
The Crucifixion of Jesus

As the moon reflects the light of the sun, so the accounts of the crucifixion reflect the presence of the Light incarnate in Jesus. When we look carefully at the details of the gospel story, an apparent triumph of the forces of evil over the forces of good is completely transformed. Mark's gospel gives us the first written account of that transformation.

The Darkness before the Dawn

Shortly after Jesus is nailed to the cross, Mark reports that "there was a great darkness at noon" (Mark 15:33). This seemingly ominous detail is actually a sign of hope, such as the dawn breaking into a dark night. According to prophecies in the Hebrew Scriptures (Joel 3, for example) this is just the kind of sign expected to accompany the arrival of the" Day of the Lord."

Even Jesus' apparent cry of despair—"My God, my God, why have you abandoned me?" (Mark 15:34)—is a sign that Jesus senses victory is near. His words are the first line of Psalm 22, a classic psalm of lament. In this type of prayer the psalmist begins by crying out all of his or her troubles, confident that God cares and is listening. The lament ends with an expression of firm belief in God's ultimate triumph (Psalm 22:28–32).

The Torn Veil

One of the most meaningful events of this first Good Friday, however, is a small detail that is easily missed. Mark informs us that at the very moment Jesus dies, "the veil of the sanctuary was torn in two from top to bottom" (Mark 15:38). The veil Mark refers to is the curtain separating the vestibule in the Temple building in Jerusalem from the "Holy of Holies" located in the rear of the structure. This back room was the most sacred spot on earth for Jesus and his contemporaries because this was believed to be the spot where God resided. For all Jews, including those who would come to accept Jesus as Messiah and Son of God, that curtain represented the fundamental gap between the fullness of God's glory and the faint spark of that glory within humanity.

No one in Mark's intended audience of Jewish Christians could have missed the significance of what it meant for that Temple curtain to be removed. The moment of Jesus' death on the cross marks the beginning of a new world order in which, as the words of the Christmas song say, "God and sinner [are] reconciled." And in the person of the Holy Spirit, God is closer to each of us than even the unspoken yearnings of our hearts.

For Thought and Discussion

1. Reflect on a time when you went out of your way to help someone simply because you wanted to and not because you had to do so. How did it feel? What happened as a result?

2. What are the signs of hope you see in your own ministry as a catechist? Be as specific as you possibly can be.

3. Imagine yourself at the foot of the cross. (Read Mark 15 for inspiration.) If you had one question to ask of Jesus, or one thing to say, what would it be?

4. Introduce your students to the details of the crucifixion account by having them produce a front page of a newspaper that reviews the events of Holy Week. (Sample headline: "Security increased dramatically as acclaimed prophet enters Jerusalem.") Provide large sheets of paper, markers, pens, pencils, etc. Let your students provide the imagination.

5. The crucifixion, if presented to young children at all, must be presented with great sensitivity. One way of dealing with the essential theme is to ask children to think about a time when they were willing to give up something they liked because they wanted to help someone else. (Examples: sharing a toy with a friend; turning the TV off to play a game with their younger siblings.) Children could illustrate their stories, and individual drawings/art projects could be collected to make a class collage.

40

The Resurrection:
The Light of Christ

"When it was already dawn, Jesus was standing on the shore; but the disciples did not realize that it was Jesus" (John 21:4). All of the gospels proclaim the resurrection of Jesus through stories that contain great hope. In John's gospel, however, this proclamation of hope and joy is explicitly wrapped in a visual symbol of light. In the above verse from the story of Jesus' post-resurrection appearance in Galilee, the break of dawn signals not just the arrival of the sun in the sky but of the Son of God.

John introduces the theme of light breaking into darkness in the very beginning of his gospel (1:5). The contrast between dark and light continues on both a literal level and a symbolic level throughout the story. Only John tells us that "it was night" as Judas heads out from the Last Supper to carry out his dark deed of betrayal (13:30). Even as Mary Magdalene makes her way to the tomb in which Jesus' body had been laid (it was early on the morning of the third day after the crucifixion), the darkness emanating from that tragic event still holds her in its grip (John 20:1).

The Light Begins to Appear

Things change quickly, however. By the time Mary has fled from the empty tomb and returned with Peter and the "disciple whom Jesus loved," the two men have enough light to see that Jesus' burial clothes are empty and neatly tucked away (20:3–7). This early dawning of both the sunlight and the good news of the resurrection is enough to convince the beloved disciple that something wonderful has happened—but Mary needs more. As the two men return home she remains outside the tomb, weeping, still trapped in her grief (20:8–11).

Two heavenly beings bathed in light now appear to her and set the stage for the event that will fill Mary's soul with the light of Jesus' presence. She first mistakes a stranger in the garden for the custodian—then he calls to her by name. This is Jesus (20:12–18)! Mary can now proclaim to the other disciples, "I have seen the Lord."

Thomas Steps into the Light

The last to step into the light is Thomas. He is not present when Jesus appears to the rest of the disciples on the evening of that first Easter Sunday. Walking only by the light of human reason "doubting" Thomas says "Unless I see the mark of the nails in his hands and put my hand into his side, I will not believe" (20:25).

Exactly one week later, Thomas' senses, mind, and heart receive the light of Christ's presence and all of his doubts dissolve. Jesus' last words to Thomas remind all who read the gospel in faith that the light of the risen Christ burns brightly within them: "Blessed are those who have not seen and have believed" (John 20:29).

For Thought and Discussion

1. Do you believe that you are destined to live eternally in commu-
    nion with God and with all of the faithful departed in a fullness
    of life we cannot imagine? How does it make you feel? Does it
    affect the way you look at you life in any significant way?

2. Who and what are the sources of light in your life? Take a
    moment to appreciate them.

3. Write the sentence "Jesus is the light of the world" on the board.
    Invite the children in your group to explain what this means by
    listing the good things that light brings us. Think about how light
    dispels darkness in the Easter season and in the springtime.

4. As an extension of the previous exercise, erase the end of the
    above sentence so that it just says "Jesus is…" Invite your chil-
    dren to think of descriptive phrases to complete the sentence
    (example: "Jesus is my friend").

5. Light a candle and invite your children or teens to close their
    eyes and to quiet themselves. Read the story from John 20:1–
    18, when Mary Magdalene discovers Jesus outside of the empty
    tomb, or John 21:1–14, when Jesus appears to the disciples on
    the beach. Ask those you teach to imagine themselves in the
    role of Mary, Peter, or another disciple. When the meditation
    is over, have them describe how they felt or what they thought
    about while doing the exercise.

Epilogue

As a conclusion to this book of Bible stories, I present a story of my own. No profound insights here, and certainly no divine revelation!

Yet perhaps I can offer a small example of how humbling and glorious that sacred enterprise of catechesis can be.

Confessions of a
"Wannabe" Catechist

A few years ago, my wife was out of town for a few days. This meant that she would not be able to teach her usual second-grade religious education class at our parish. She asked me if I would drive our daughter to the session that day. Not only would I drive her, I said, but I'll even teach the lesson. After all, I've been teaching high school religious education for twenty years now. How hard could it be? Such were my thoughts.

On the day of the session, I spent a little time going over the text and preparing a lesson on the Ten Commandments. Finally I was all set to go, notes in hand, carrying a plastic dinosaur I was planning to use as part of my presentation. I set off that fateful Wednesday afternoon to impart my pearls of wisdom to a group of eager seven- and eight-year-olds.

The Storm Warning

I should have picked up on the first storm warning when I entered the room. The aide who helps my wife said, "You probably want to keep John and Arnold separated." However I'm a "Professional Teacher" after all, so I figured whatever came up I could handle. Nevertheless, before our session began, I firmly but calmly insisted that the two boys sit apart from one another.

Arnold was really not happy with this arrangement. I said, "Okay, boys and girls, let's talk about the most special gifts we have ever received"—my way of beginning a lesson on the commandments as God's gift. Arnold purposefully started to fold the stack of papers in front of him into a squadron of airplanes. Seeing that the boy's act of civil disobedience was peaceful at the moment, I thought it best just to watch and see if he would make any attempt to launch the planes. (He never did.)

After beginning with my own story about a plastic dinosaur as a special gift I received one Christmas, I invited each child to share his or her tale about a favorite gift. Most of the children responded enthusiastically. John was so enthusiastic that he must have named at least ten gifts before I stopped counting. He probably would have come up with several hundred more, real or imagined, if I hadn't suggested we move on to the next child.

Unexpected Antics

When everyone was seated, I said, "I want to show you something on the board." As I turned toward the blackboard to point out the sentence I had written there, I saw that John was no longer in his seat. He was busy feeding his pen to the plastic dinosaur.

"I don't think dinosaurs like to eat pens, John," I said, attempting to massage my now fraying nerves with some humor. It worked. John left the dinosaur alone and returned to his seat.

Next, he climbed on top of his desk. I've been told that during the time I was coaxing John back down, Arnold began hitting himself in the head with his book, but honestly I don't remember.

Still, all things considered, I felt that session was progressing well. Everyone participated. The other children were really attentive. When the bell rang for the end of the session, I thought I had done a pretty good job.

The Brutal Truth

"Dad," my daughter said as the children began to leave, "I need to talk to you."

"Sure, honey," I responded. "What is it?"

She paused for a moment. "Dad," she said, "you have to learn to be more strict with those boys."

I was stunned. I turned to my assistant for support. Surely an adult could see the subtle yet skillful mastery of my teaching. "What did you think?" I asked.

She shrugged. "Well," she began, trying to break the news as gently as she could, "those boys are really hard to handle. And, after all, you are a substitute teacher."

So there it was. The brutal truth. Maybe I was a legend in my own mind, but to that particular group of second graders on that particular afternoon, I was merely, "the Sub." To slightly paraphrase a line from an old Johnny Cash song ("A Boy Named Sue"), I stumbled from that classroom not so tall and not so proud.

The Gifts I Received

Besides a lesson in humility, however, I left that session with a few other gifts. I received more smiles per minute from that happy little group than I can remember seeing in even my most enthusiastic high school class. Most of all, I gained a much more profound respect for the thousands of catechists who give so freely of their time and talent each week. In doing so, they provide a unique and powerful witness to the meaning of discipleship.

As my children and I headed to the parking lot, one of the other boys came up to me wearing a smile as wide as his face. "Can I see the dinosaur?" he asked. While we spent a quiet moment connecting with one another through a common interest, I decided to become involved in catechesis on a more regular basis. The sixth or seventh grade might be nice.

Postscript: Since the time I wrote this piece I have become a full-time catechist for the eighth grade in my parish. The good news is, no one has ever climbed on a desk. But, oh, that texting!